# THE
# Turnaround Manager's
## HANDBOOK

# THE
# Turnaround Manager's
## HANDBOOK

BY RICHARD S. SLOMA

**BeardBooks**
Washington, D.C.

Library of Congress Cataloging-in-Publication Data

Sloma, Richard S.
    The turnaround manager's handbook / Richard S. Sloma.
       p.   cm.
    Previous ed. published: New York: Free Press, c1985.
    Includes index.
    ISBN 1-893122-40-9
    1. Industrial management. 2. Corporate reorganizations. I. Title

HD31 .S5774 1999
658.4'063--dc21                              99-051399

Copyright 1985 by the Free Press, A Division of Macmillan, Inc.
Reprinted 2000 by Beard Books, Washington, D.C.

All rights reserved. No part of this publication may be reproduced, stored in a retrieval system, or transmitted in any form, by any means, without the prior written consent of the publisher.

Printed in the United States of America

With devotion and love to Dee—
my wife, friend, sweetheart, and confidante—
without whose patience, understanding, and love
*none* of the turnarounds in my life
would have been successfully managed.

# CONTENTS

| | |
|---|---|
| LIST OF FIGURES | *vii* |
| PREFACE | *ix* |
| INTRODUCTION: What This Book Is All About and How Best to Use It | *xi* |
| OVERVIEW: Just Thirteen Steps to Success! | *1* |

## SECTIONS

| | | |
|---|---|---|
| I. | What Is a Turnaround? | *11* |
| II. | What Is a Successful Turnaround? | *27* |
| III. | Symptoms of the Type of Turnaround | *39* |
| IV. | Diagnostic, Analytical Tools | *69* |
| V. | Remedial, Restorative Action | *121* |
| VI. | The Operating Organization—Key to Turnaround Success | *187* |

## APPENDIXES

| | | |
|---|---|---|
| 1. | Complete Catalog of Key Symptoms | *205* |
| 2. | Kit of Macro-Tools | *207* |

| | | |
|---|---|---|
| 3. | Kit of Micro-Tools | *208* |
| 4. | Arsenal of Remedial, Restorative Actions | *211* |
| 5. | Action/Symptom/Analytical Tool Interreference Table | *213* |
| 6. | Action/Turnaround Stage Relevance Charts | *216* |

INDEX *225*

# LIST OF FIGURES

1. Turnaround Management Flowchart (Overview)    *2*
2. Burden Expense Symptom Anatomy (Section III)    *53*
3. Engineering Expense Symptom Anatomy (Section III)    *58*
4. Analysis of Change in Operating Pre-Tax (Section VI)    *194*

Charts for Actions 1 through 31 (Appendix 6)    *219*

# PREFACE

Far too many otherwise competent managers mistakenly believe that a turnaround means a firm that is on the verge of going down the tubes! The true nature of a turnaround is a firm whose recent past or projected future financial performance is unacceptable to the owners/creditors. The turnaround malaise is dissected into its four stages of progressive virulence. Using the analogy of restoration of *physical health* to the restoration of *fiscal health*, this *Handbook* presents detailed discussions of the following topics:

How to examine the corporate patient

How to perform an accurate diagnosis

How to infer the proper prognosis

How to prescribe only the required treatment and therapy

Devoid of frivolous and fatuous generalities, this *Handbook* deals exclusively with the quantitative operational specifics that the professional turnaround manager must utilize for success. The "company doctor" is supplied with complete details of the twenty-eight symptoms and the forty-eight analytical tools with which to measure and diagnose the firm's ills accurately. The "company doctor" is next armed with the thirty-one remedial, restorative actions which provide pinpoint, relevant, and effective curative treatment, tailored to the diagnosis. The turnaround manager will avoid "management by thrashabout" and retain the baby intact while disposing of every drop of bathwater.

Finally, the "company doctor" learns specifically how to motivate—and to monitor the progress of—the operating organization so that it will vigorously and enthusiastically perform the prescribed treatment and therapy. A uniquely innovative planning technique is presented which discretely measures the incremental improvement in operating performance required to insure enduring corporate health.

The author has cogently distilled more than twenty years of successful hands-on operating management experience in this compact, "meat-and-potatoes," easily usable *Handbook.*

# INTRODUCTION

*What This Book Is All About
and How Best to Use It*

An accurate subtitle for this book could be, "How to Become a Successful Company Doctor." The analogy really isn't all that bad. A company in need of turnaround action is a financially "sick" company. Just as the best that a human patient can do is to imperfectly inform the human doctor of what that patient thinks the symptoms are, so too, the company records, alone, can only imperfectly reveal its symptoms in its financial and operating records. Just as the human doctor must complete a diagnosis from critical evaluation and testing of the symptoms, and from the logical inferences derived from that analysis, so too must the management charged with responsibility for the fiscal health of the firm evaluate, test, measure, and draw logical inferences of not only symptom cause, but treatment as well.

The procedure is remarkably coincident. First, document the history of the patient's financial health condition. Second, perform an examination of the patient to identify and quantify the symptoms. Third, apply interpretational judgment and expertise to those findings in order to complete the diagnosis. Fourth, prescribe remedial treatment such that the prognosis, if at all possible, is favorable. Fifth, perform periodic checkups to monitor performance and make appropriate prescriptive adjustments.

This *Handbook,* then, is aimed at the corporate general practitioner and those who so aspire. Far too often turnaround books either focus only on a particular problem (e.g., loss of market share) or only on a particular treatment (e.g., reduce personnel). Too many turnaround books are aimed at one or another group of specialists. A direct consequence is that if the particular company patient that you are treating does not have the particular symptoms or warrants "special" treatment, not only are you, as the practitioner, out of luck—so also is your company patient!

Management experts, so-called, tend far too often to make the management of turnarounds sound more complicated than it really is. No surprise. It's ego serving to portray yourself as the master of the mysterious and esoteric. And besides, if you can get away with it, it can increase your salary and bonus.

The plain, unvarnished truth is that successful turnaround management is startlingly simple. It consists simply of heavy and sustained doses of common sense and hard, ofttimes tedious work. This *Handbook* can help develop the former—the latter, as you very well know, is up to you.

By the way, this *Handbook,* as you will soon see, talks a lot about data, analyses, and documentation. There are a lot of specifics. The greatest compliment I have thus far received about this *Handbook* (and I really don't think it can be topped) was, "You call for a whole bunch of data and data analysis. For Cris'sake Sloma, if we already had all this information and had some idea how to use it, we wouldn't be in trouble in the first place!" That, my friend, is precisely the point!

Prudent study of the *Handbook* will enable you to confidently prescribe the effective cure of *any* turnaround situation. Only effective cures are dealt with, however. The goal is to restore the firm to financial health which is best defined as generation of an enduring and robust stream of quality profits and cash flow. What we, as professional practitioners, seek to do is to enhance the enduring value of the shareholders' investment. You will find no superficial, "make it look good," facelifts in *this* book!

As you will learn in detail in Section II, successful turnaround treatment is a tailored, customized restorative program. While some symptoms may be shared by different stages of turnarounds, effective treatment is dependent upon accurate differentiation and selection of only those that are relevant to our specific patient. Similarly, the treatment to be prescribed must relate directly to the true symptoms. Finally, one must be able to select the restorative or remedial action properly. In order to make that selection successfully, the results of various diagnostic and prognostic tests (our corporate analytical tools) must be both thorough and accurate.

Thus, <u>The Turnaround Manager's Handbook</u> provides a complete explanation of the four stages of a turnaround, the twenty-eight symptoms of the need for turnaround treatment, forty-eight analytical tools you will need to insure that only effective treatment is prescribed, and the thirty-one remedial actions or treatments to restore the financial health of the firm.

Finally, you will learn how to mobilize the operating organization to insure that the prescribed treatment will be administered with dedication, commitment, and perseverance.

Unlike my earlier book, *No-Nonsense Management* (Macmillan, 1977), in which I encouraged the reader to dip into it most anywhere his interest had been piqued, this *Handbook* is meant to be first read from beginning to end. The succeeding sections build upon previous ones, so that the best use will be made if you follow straight through in your first reading. After that first reading, keep this *Handbook* on your desk so that you can quickly and easily refresh yourself as seeming "new" situations arise.

I've tried my very best to keep this *Handbook* free from fluff. There's already far too much in business management literature. To the extent that there still is some of that stuff, please forgive me. I'll try harder in my next book.

## OVERVIEW

# JUST THIRTEEN STEPS TO SUCCESS!

This might be considered the most important section of this *Handbook*. If you fail to grasp and understand this overview, anything else you do will be at best suboptimal, and at worst counterproductive. The essence of the professional approach to a turnaround is captured in Figure 1. It consists of only thirteen steps. Not only is competent execution of each step essential, the sequence of the execution is equally critical.

Let's walk through the algorithm, step-by-step, to insure that you can get a firm grasp of every ingredient of a successful turnaround. The first step is to quantify the twenty-eight symptoms. Section III presents full explanatory detail of each of them. Usually, many of the symptoms can be quantified from the firm's accounting and operational records. A distinction must be made between the time frames within which each symptom must be evaluated. From the historical records, the "run-rate" values can be relatively easily determined. While examina-

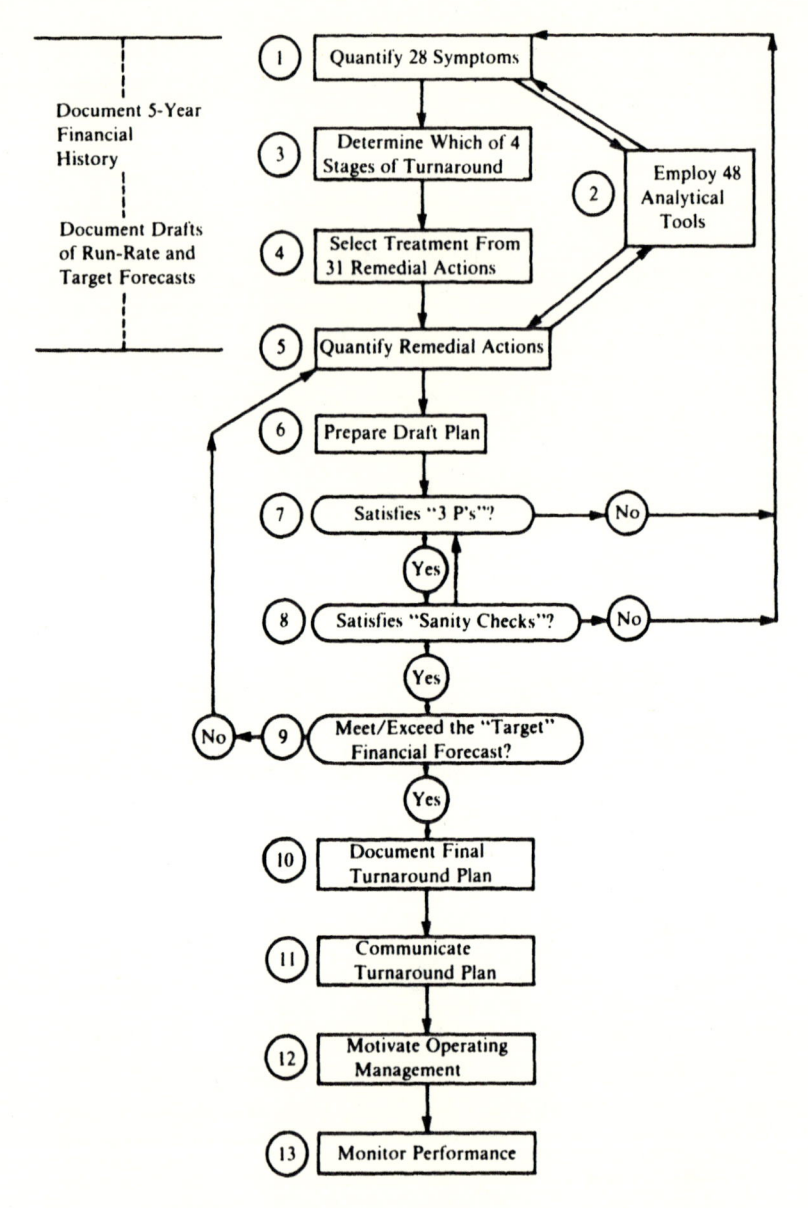

**Figure 1. Turnaround Management Flowchart**

tion of the historical records will yield an understanding of where the firm has been and the trend of behavior of the symptoms, the much more useful time frame for turnaround analytical purposes is the forecast of symptom behavior.

And, of prime importance from among the array of forecasts is the "forward-aged margin dollar content in the order backlog" (see Section IV). This series of numbers tells us how much or how little pre-tax profit is available for us to work with in the near or measurable future before impact of the traditional "below the line" expenses for administration, finance/accounting, sales/marketing and, very often, engineering. If the data are available by product line, even if they are approximated, so much the better. The amount of pre-tax profit available, even at the factory level, provides highly useful insight into the imminence of financial disaster. This measure is also one of the truly key tools with which to monitor performance as remedial action is taken. It gives us a unique "early warning" capability.

Don't despair because there are twenty-eight symptoms to quantify. It may seem that there are too many and it will take too much time to quantify them. There is a danger of contracting paralysis by analysis. Evaluation of each of the twenty-eight *is* needed so that improper identification of the type of turnaround will be avoided. Many of the symptoms can be rather quickly quantified, depending upon the state of the firm's accounting and operational records. Also, many can be concurrently quantified. Only rarely is the quantification of one symptom dependent upon the earlier quantification of another.

In short, with rare exception, they do not have to be processed sequentially.

Once the twenty-eight symptoms have been quantified, forty-eight analytical tools are provided so that the proper inferences can be drawn from the symptom data. All forty-eight tools are discussed in detail in Section V. Note that there is not a one-to-one match-up between symptoms and analytical tools. Some symptom inferences require the use of several analytical tools; and conversely, some analytical tools are used with more than one symptom. And it may be the case that, for the particular firm we are facing, some of the tools may be irrelevant. Caveat: before you decide to set aside one or another analytical tool, be doubly sure that the cost/benefit of its use is clearly disadvantageous. As a rule, you will always be better off by using all of the tools rather than not.

Note that the analytical tools are used twice. In both instances, they are used in quantification steps—first for the symptoms, and second for remedial actions. Their use is similar in both cases. Namely, careful use of the analytical tools will assure that (1) proper inferences are drawn from the examination of the symptoms and (2) proper, i.e., relevant and effective, remedial actions are selected.

Throughout this *Handbook*, you will encounter the concept and use of "inferences." Because managing a turnaround requires competence in drawing logical, useful, practical, relevant, measurable inferences, let's make sure that we understand each other. Webster tells us that to "infer" means to deduce; to judge; to conclude. He goes on, "Infer implies arriving at a conclusion by reasoning from evidence; implies arriving at a logically necessary conclusion at the end of a chain of reasoning."

Turnaround management demands very heavy doses of "arriving at a logically necessary conclusion at the end of a chain of reasoning." Let's talk about the evidence upon which you will rely while building your chain of reasoning. Evidence means a great deal more than merely facts. Facts will be supplied to you as you quantify the symptoms of the firm. Transforming those facts into evidence requires the application of analytical tools to put flesh on the bones, to highlight characteristics, to capture nuances, and to unravel subtleties.

It is *after* symptoms have been subjected to processing with analytical tools that "evidence" is first available to you. Anything prior can, at best, be only an opinion. Only when evidence is available to you can you begin to build a "chain of reasoning" from which useful, professional inferences can be drawn. A successful turnaround manager is, first, a successful builder of chains of reasoning!

Yet, nonquantitative inferences are worse than useless, particularly when you're selecting the remedial actions in Step 4. Here, the remedial action, alone, is a "fact"—yes, the firm would, indeed, be better off if the indirect personnel population were reduced. But, to convert this fact into evidence from which a practical, manageable turnaround plan of action can be inferred, the application again of analytical tools is mandatory.

Drawing an inference amounts to reasoning such as: if "A" is (probably) true, then "B" is also (probably) true. And, given "B," then "C" (very probably) will be true, too. Such is the stuff of which inferential chains are made. This *Handbook* helps you not only to identify the "A's," "B's," "C's," and so on, it will help you to assess and assign degrees of probability to them as they are encountered in the real turnaround world. Inference is reasoned anticipation. Reasoned anticipation is a necessary ingredient in the make-up of a successful company doctor.

In Step 3, the determination of the stage of turnaround is made by deduction from symptom measurements and values. It may be that you will, on occasion, face more than one stage at the same time. The approach presented here will enable you to distinguish between and among them so that only the appropriate remedial actions will be identified and executed. Detailed discussion of the four stages of turnarounds is presented in Section I.

Optimize use of the time that it takes to complete Steps 1, 2, 3, and 4 by beginning work on Step 5 concurrently. The drafts should be completed for both the run-rate forecast and the target forecast. Even though they may not yet be final, if diligently pursued they will closely approximate the final versions.

These two forecasts, and the "differences" between them, the resultant objective forecast, will prove to be of inestimable value as you quantify the remedial actions in Step 5. The objective forecast will serve as a limiting influence on the extent, timing, and depth of action that you plan to take. It will serve to insure that you do keep the baby and dispose only of the bathwater, as you will learn in detail in Section V.

Once our examination has progressed from quantification of symptoms to identification of stage of turnaround, we are in position to prescribe remedial actions. Thus, Step 4 calls for selection from among thirty-one remedial actions. In Section V you will learn, in detail, which remedial actions relate to (i.e., are most useful with) each of the four stages of turnaround. This step is crucial. Once the gravity of the situation facing the firm has been quantified, there will be a strong temptation to plunge immediately into action. Patience—NOT procrastination—is essential. Careful matching of remedial actions, of therapy, to the measured symptoms will assure an effective cure in as timely a manner as possible.

In order to translate the chosen remedial actions into an effective, measurable, and communicable turnaround plan, the remedial actions *must* be quantified. Be mindful that the output of this step is not so much the quantification of the remedial action itself. The desired output is, rather, the quantification of the timing and dollar effect of relatively successful implementation of that action. What we seek to reduce to calendarized amounts are the probable, realistic, and most likely results of the prescribed action. By analogy, this step is akin to the prognosis, "If you really stick to this diet, you will lose four to six pounds in the first ten days and fifteen to twenty pounds in thirty days."

Once again, too, we employ the forty-eight analytical tools. The prognosis is (or should be) expressed in the same language as that used to define the symptoms. Thus, as action is taken, progress of the cure can be expressed in the same terms as the symptoms so that recovery can be handily monitored as mitigation of the symptoms increases.

Arriving at Step 6, the draft plan can now be finalized. Note that it is "finalized" in Step 10, not only just begun. Actually a number of plan elements will already have been sufficiently quantified as Steps 1 through 5 are completed. The prime function of Step 6 is to correlate the outputs of Steps 1 through 5 and transform them into a cohesive, convincing, understandable, communicable, measurable, monitorable, relevant, and restorative set of numbers and prose that will, at once, motivate operating management to meet/exceed the financial objectives and provide a rational basis for owners and creditors to withhold disinvestment and credit call action.

Steps 1 through 5 are essentially analytical. Step 6 is the first attempt at synthesis. In Steps 1 through 5 we anatomized the operational and organizational performance of the firm. We broke down the elements to crystallize the unshakeable facts; we employed analytical skills and talents. In Step 6, we employ creative skills and talents. See *No-Nonsense Planning* (Free Press, 1984) to learn, in detail, the power of plans and how to get your plan approved.

Step 7 is the first effectiveness filter through which our turnaround plan must pass. The purpose of Steps 7 and 8 is to interrogate our plan deeply and rigorously enough such that we are confident of both its relevance and its materiality; that it will indeed achieve that which is necessary to be achieved. Step 7 focuses our attention on the "Three P's"—people, product, and plant—which are treated in considerable detail in Section I. What we ask is, "Does our plan properly consider all Three P's? Will management of the Three P's be sufficiently enhanced to assure a successful turnaround?" If the answer to any of our questions is "No," we must go all the way back to Step 1—we do not yet adequately understand the firm's symptoms. If the answers are "Yes," we proceed to Step 8 where we apply the sanity checks as highlighted in Section IV and in detail in *No-Nonsense Planning*. The purpose of Step 8 is to insure that the selected remedial actions are in conformance with operational constraints and relationships. If they are not, we again return to Step 1 for a reassessment of the symptoms. A reassessment of the Three P's is also indicated to ascertain whether the Three P's criteria have been sufficiently modified to accommodate remedial actions which exceed initial Three P's capabilities.

If the sanity checks are satisfied, we proceed to Step 9 which is covered in Sections II and IV of this *Handbook*. Here we ask whether there is sufficient probability that acceptable financial results will eventuate from execution of the identified remedial actions. If the answer is "No," we return to Step 5 to requantify the remedial actions. We ask questions such as, "Are there *additional* opportunities for cost-expense reduction? Can we *further* increase sales?" and so on. It is noteworthy that the "Step 5–Step 9–Step 5–Step 9 . . ." reiteration cycle is usually the most time-consuming in the entire effort.

If the answer to Step 9 is (finally), "Yes," we can proceed to Step 10 to document the final plan. This step is presented more completely in Section V of this *Handbook*, and most completely in *No-Nonsense Planning.* The output of Step 10 should be *the* set of documents that embody the specific, quantified, measurable planned remedial actions which, when properly executed, will most likely result in financial performance such that (1) the firm will survive and (2) the requirements of the owners and the creditors will be met.

Merely having a set of documents, no matter if all of it is totally relevant, substantive, and most probably effective, is not enough. Nothing favorable can begin to happen until the plan is communicated. It must be communicated *externally* so that the concerns of the owners and creditors can be assuaged. But, and maybe even more importantly, the plan must be communicated *internally* so that operating management can perform.

Finally, Steps 12 and 13 are, and really should be, considered together. Motivating operating management and monitoring performance are inseparable activities. Before one can offer valid congratulations for successful progress, one must be able to define the results of that effort objectively, impersonally, and measurably. In addition to the discussion of these two vital steps in Section VI, the serious company doctor will find in-depth reference to *No-Nonsense Management* (Macmillan, 1977) and *How to Measure Managerial Performance* (Macmillan, 1980) to be of remarkable value.

# SECTION I

# WHAT IS A TURNAROUND?

A "turnaround" can refer either to a business firm that faces financial disaster or action taken to prevent the occurrence of that financial disaster. An example of the former might be "The ABC company is a turnaround situation." Of the latter one might say, "They successfully turned the XYZ company around." Occasionally, an individual is termed a "turnaround expert." What is meant is that the person faced a turnaround situation and took actions such that the predicted dire financial consequences were avoided.

A turnaround situation is first recognized when there is serious concern or dissatisfaction with the firm's performance, results, and/or near-term forecasts of performance and results. Usually, it is the firm's creditors who first become aware of the problem, whether they are "formal" creditors such as banks and other similar lending institutions, or "informal" creditors such as vendors whose invoice payments are long overdue. If the firm is publicly held, the turnaround alarm is sometimes rung by the shareholders, the owners. Only rarely is it the incumbent management who brings the presence of turnaround jeopardy to light.

A common misconception is that *all* turnarounds consist of or deal with transforming an unprofitable firm into a profitable one. Not so! It just seems that way because too many managers allow the firm to deteriorate to that unforgivable point. And, those turnarounds which get the most publicity are those that involve a shift from red to black. Yet the greatest rewards should really go to those managers who take their firm from grey to ebony.

A true sign of managerial professionalism is when, early on, the operating management discern that the firm's profitability is or soon will be less than acceptable. Unfortunately, the chief operating officers who see to it that *their* firm doesn't become unprofitable fail to get the favorable press notice that they truly and richly deserve. *Fortune* magazine would do well, indeed, if they featured the "Top 100 Chief Operating Officers," instead of focusing exclusively on CEOs! If the truth were known, it is the COOs who make the CEOs look good. If operating performance is excellent, the CEO gets to take the public bows—because, so the story goes, he had the wisdom to select the "right" COO. If, on the other hand, operating performance is poor to lousy, the COO walks the plank while the CEO accepts the resignation—which, by the way, is always for "personal" reasons, policy differences, or to pursue other (always unspecified) interests—with regret in varying degrees of intensity.

Turnarounds include those firms that only generate an *unacceptable* flow of cash and profit. Sure, the firm is profitable all right, but just not profitable enough. And even further, as we shall see a little later, a firm can be ripe for a turnaround even if the only sign of financial trouble is a cloud on the horizon. That is, there is credible forecast evidence that the cash/profit flow most probably *will* become unacceptable at some future period.

In brief, turnarounds exist in an infinite variety of shades and hues. As a professional corporate practitioner, you must not only be aware of, but must be able to cope with, all of them.

Upon reflection, it is not at all surprising that incumbent management is the least likely origin of turnaround recognition. Turnaround situations are only extremely rarely thrust upon firms by outside, uncontrollable forces. Almost without exception, turnaround situations arise because of management's incompetence, ineptness, carelessness, ego, and/or inexpertise. It is simply too much to ask or expect incumbent management to be objective in evaluations of past performance and near-term likely performance when they are the very same people who, by mismanagement, allowed the firm's financial health to deteriorate in the first place.

If a firm faces a turnaround situation, it is usually the case that incumbent management caused the situation to develop by a combination of imprudent action and inaction. Management failed to properly and professionally pay enough attention to the "Three P's." Any firm's success, or lack of it, can be traced to the way that the Three P's were managed or mismanaged.

## THE THREE P'S

*The first P is people.* It is the operational management and supervisory group of people of whom I speak. If the firm faces a turnaround situation, there is probably a glaring lack of effective planning and control procedures. If such procedures had ever somehow been documented, they probably have become outdated and they certainly were not consistently enforced.

Another reliable inference is that the management or supervisory group did not have suitable incentive to perform at higher than only indifferent levels. They commonly have only a vague idea of the financial status of the firm and its objectives. Generally too, they have only a myopic view and understanding of their duties and responsibilities as managers. They incorrectly view their day-to-day functional performance as the totality of their responsibility. They focus on the efficiency with which they daily process papers—orders, invoices, receiving reports, inspection forms, and so on—rather than on the effectiveness with which the firm meets and beats competition.

The greater the prevalence with which one encounters an attitude of "It's not my job," the sooner the turnaround situation will ripen. The greater the lack of identity of job performance to cash flow and pre-tax performance of the firm, the sooner the turnaround alarm will sound. Yet the entire group of management/supervisory personnel is hardly indictable. It is, rather, top management—

the chief executive and chief operating officers—who are principally accountable, whether they accept it or not.

Two of my earlier books, *No-Nonsense Management* (Macmillan, 1977) and *How To Measure Managerial Performance* (Macmillan, 1979), deal in detail with actions and attitudes which will avoid mismanagement of the first P, people.

*The second P is product.* If the firm's product contributes to the severity of the turnaround situation, the firm's management has failed to adapt it properly to changing market needs. A basic product law is, "The most successful product is that which most successfully solves the user's problems." That law has not been, nor will it ever be repealed!

There are only three aspects of product to which management must devote itself. Because there are only three, it is sadly amazing how frequently one or more of them is simply ignored. The management somehow become convinced that they are more knowledgeable than the market they seek to serve. A sad example: A firm, entering the home security market, learned from professional market surveys that the public in general was not willing to pay more than $1000 per installation. Then, for totally erroneous and only rationalistic excuses, the firm's management, *after* significant investment, decided that they knew better. At bottom, it turned out, was their misguided commitment to the idea that price *must* be a mark-up from cost rather than what the market told them it must be. They launched the business at a price of $1395! No surprises. Insufficient sales ensued. Solely because of management ego, the firm's financial performance suffered, along with minority shareholders, for nearly two years before the bleeding was stopped by sale of the business at a deep discount.

The first aspect of product is price. The price to the customer must be low enough so that it is less than the cost of his problem. Yet, the price must be high enough so that it exceeds product cost by enough to yield an acceptable rate of return on the investment needed to produce and sell the product. Further, the product cost must not be allowed to escalate to the point where the margin it brings to the firm becomes so low that it contributes to the creation of a turnaround situation. A portion of product cost too often overlooked or slighted, for example, is the post-sale cost of warranty.

The second aspect of the firm's product is quality. First, the product's quality must be sufficiently high to meet all applicable statutory, regulatory, and/or trade custom requirements. Second, quality must be high enough that the user maintenance cost does not outweigh the benefit of problem solution. On the other hand, the cost of quality must not be allowed to grow to the extent that return of profitable margin is jeopardized. Too often it is the case that design and manufacturing engineers overdesign in their quest for the "perfect" product. Significant material cost reduction was achieved by a valve manufacturer when product design specifications were lowered to two times the ASME (American Society of Mechanical Engineers) requirement from the five to ten times that the engineers had earlier established.

The third aspect of product is availability. It is sometimes called delivery cycle time, other times it's called service. Of course, if a user has a problem and you have a product that can satisfactorily solve that problem, the user wants it sooner rather than later. Because the product solution offers a favorable benefit/cost ratio to the user, timely delivery of product (and the follow-on parts sales) is of value to the customer/user. The initial tendency of the firm's management is to satisfy the availability aspect of product by increasing investment in finished goods inventory. However, if investment in inventory becomes too high, that action alone *can* precipitate the most severe stage of turnaround, the cash crunch.

Another caveat regarding finished goods inventory: Prudent investment in finished goods inventory is inversely related to the amount of technological or engineering content in *each* unit of product. Please refer to *No-Nonsense Planning* (Free Press, 1984) for detailed discussion of this and other "sanity checks."

*The third of the Three P's is plant.* This includes the physical plant, equipment, and ancillary facilities (warehousing, etc.) with which the firm produces its product. There are, again, only three principal aspects relevant to turnaround situations. Safety of the employees cannot be overlooked. On the one hand, it is felt that the firm cannot spend (invest) too much money to ensure employee safety. Yet the cost of safety must be compared to safety cost. In other words, the minimum spending level is that which ensures that the plant is operated in compliance with statutory, regulatory, and other contractual obligations. It is generally the case that spending beyond that minimum level fails to reap an acceptable incremental return from reduction in insurance premiums and related costs.

Obsolescence of plant can be both a problem and an opportunity. While product costs tend to rise as obsolescence becomes more pervasive, product costs generally do not fall consistent with reduction of obsolescence UNLESS the new investments also provide a measurable improvement in productivity. Merely replacing an old, obsolete, poorly laid out warehouse, for example, with a spanking-new, poorly laid out warehouse gains nothing at all. Replacing a worn out belt-driven lathe with a new belt-driven lathe may reduce unit labor cost—but only trivially at best. Replacing a worn out belt-driven lathe (or, better, several of them) with one electronically controlled machining center not only offers significant reductions in unit labor cost, but may actually create opportunities for reductions also in unit material cost.

While these two aspects of plant may offer some turnaround benefits, they are only a fraction of the benefits available by judicious redeployment of plant capacity. Capacity is a measure of the volume of product that can be produced in a practical fashion in a practical time frame. Only rarely is a plant capable of production on a twenty-four-hour day, seven-day week basis. Infrequently, one will come upon a plant capable of production on a two-shift, five-day week basis. The principal real-world restrictions on production in excess of a single-shift, five-day week basis are shortages of labor and management/supervisory personnel. People in general simply don't like to work other than the "normal," "traditional" day shift on weekdays.

For turnaround analyses, the most useful measure of plant capacity is the output produced by the fully manned day shift of direct labor adjusted by the run-rate level of direct labor efficiency. Of course, this is an approximation. The value of using approximations in turnaround situations is explored in more detail in Section IV (Macro-Tool M2). The general rule is that the higher the ratio of actual production divided by production capacity, the lower the unit cost of the products produced. The improvement in unit cost stems almost exclusively from the greater number of product units over which the fixed, or constant, burden/overhead expenses can be spread. Variable costs, which vary with the number of units produced, tend to increase faster as production levels approach and exceed "practical" capacity as defined earlier. The principal reason is that cost penalties are incurred to encourage labor and management to work during generally undesirable hours.

In turnaround situations, there are only four plant-related strategies that can usefully be pursued. They are: consolidate, close, sell, and expand. These strategies are most effectively applied with a department-by-department implementation plan. These strategies will be explored in greater detail in Section V.

## THE FOUR STAGE CONTINUUM

As is evident from the discussion up to this point, there are a number of factors that determine or define any given turnaround situation. One or another of them may or may not be present; one or another of them may exert significant impact. Nonetheless, and despite the seeming large number of variable inputs, it turns out happily that there are, after all is said and done, only four basic stages of turnaround situations. While they each are discussed in detail in Section II, a brief overview will prove useful.

### Stage 1. Cash Crunch

Disaster is imminent. The firm has not only run out of cash, it has used up its credit line as well. Payrolls will soon go unpaid. Bankers are calling for meetings in *their* offices. (Oh, oh!) Vendors have put the firm on a COD basis. And so on.

Unfortunately, this stage is the most frequently encountered by turnaround experts. The basic reason for this prevalence is the mirrored prevalence of poor, rather than excellent, management. Too many so-called managers either cannot or will not recognize and deal with the earlier stages of financial problems.

### Stage 2. Cash Shortfall

We find here pretty much the same situation as with the cash crunch with the major exception that disaster is not all that imminent. The crunch has not yet hit, but it *is* visible to the trained eye of the professional in a three- to six-month forecast—between one and two quarters out. The principal reason why this stage is less prevalently recognized and dealt with than the cash crunch is that, if management's attention *can* be pointed at a probability three to six months out, they usually can be prodded to do something at least to alleviate the symptoms. If management, on the other hand, *regularly* really looks ahead for a couple of quarters, they probably already have the basics of turnaround avoidance pretty much in hand. The chance for deterioration to a cash crunch has been profoundly lowered.

### Stage 3. Quantity of Profit

Typically, this is the case of a firm, previously profitable, that is suffering from some erosion of profit in relatively recent times. It's not yet in a serious loss position, but six- to twelve-month forecasts reveal frequent periods of bleeding.

### Stage 4. Quality of Profit

This is the stage that is regularly addressed by professional managers. To the extent that concerted, effective early action is taken, the likelihood of facing any of the other stages is diminished. The time frame of concern is a year, often (and wisely) even longer. The tip-off is decreasing value of the ratio of the operating pre-tax divided by net sales. But let's not get too far ahead.

There are two very important features of the four stages of turnaround situations. The first is that the stages of turnarounds are NOT mutually exclusive. This becomes clear when one notes that one of the basic differences between stages is the time horizon of financial disaster for each of them. That is, failure to take remedial action in any of the situations will, sooner or later, result in financial disaster. The cardinal difference between them is the varying length of time before that unfortunate result eventuates.

The shortest time period until disaster is associated with the stage called cash crunch. The longest interval until disaster is the quality of profit stage. The other two, cash shortfall and quantity of profit have time intervals that fall roughly between the two former stages.

Effective, professional management installs and meticulously maintains planning and control systems such that performance is so well monitored that all four stages are avoided. It is always cheaper to invest in planning and control systems, and abide by their results and findings which are needed to avoid confrontation with all turnaround stages, than it is to resolve any one stage after it has arrived fully blown. Thus, part and parcel of any effective, professional turnaround plan must be inclusion of considered action relevant to each of the four stages, no matter the stage with which the firm is presently struggling.

The second feature to keep in mind is that turnaround situations only rarely develop overnight. The pervading cause of the astonishing number of instances of turnaround situations is the unwillingness and/or inability of incumbent management to recognize the many symptoms for what they really are. Unwillingness to recognize the symptoms stems from either or both of two sources. First, the ego of a person who holds the title "Manager" far too often overshadows whatever objectivity and professionalism that he or she may possess. It is difficult for all of us to admit error, but unfortunately, for too many incumbent managers it is impossible. Good money continues to be thrown after bad money until, surprise(!), there is a cash crunch on our hands.

The second source is the ostrich-like mentality of the manager, so called, who *so* fears the cessation of his or her tenure that he or she intentionally delays the day of reckoning in the futile hope that, somehow, "things will get better." The unavoidable truth is that once a firm begins to need a turnaround, things simply *don't* get better by themselves, as all truly professional managers know.

The final issue for consideration in this section can be simply stated, "Why should a firm attempt a turnaround?" The answer is deceptively simple. Because the cost (presumably to the owners) of the turnaround action is less than the cost of either (1) liquidation or (2) sale of the firm, presumably at a deep discount from book value. The answer is deceptively simple because while it is easy to put into words, I don't know of a single firm where the answer has been expressed in numbers. That is to say, I do not know of a single firm that, regularly and thoroughly, quantifies the cost of liquidation and/or the price of the firm on a distress-sale basis.

Usually it is the case that turnarounds are performed or at least started by managers upon whom the task has been thrust by the firm's creditors and/or owners. Usually also, the required results and even the prospect for those results will not soon enough be evident and the incumbents will go. No surprise, really. If they had been sufficiently competent to get the needed results, they would have taken action earlier in the first place and, thereby, precluded the need for turnaround action.

Let's not leave this topic before a sad, but crucially important fact about turnarounds is noted. Namely, turnarounds are unnecessary! They *can* be prevented. But incumbent management must be alert, dedicated, and aware of *the* cardinal principle of professional management. Yes, there is one such cardinal principle. Don't ever forget it!

It's the age-old principle that was recognized long before esoteric fads and hucksterish, "one-minute" whimsy. It is stated very simply:

## DIG THE WELL BEFORE YOU GET THIRSTY!

It makes obvious common sense, doesn't it? Of course, that's the only way to manage, isn't it? Sure, it's common sense. Sure, that's the way to manage. But then, why is it *so* often ignored? Why *are* turnarounds allowed to occur? Why can't management anticipate realistically? Why does management persist in thinking that they know better what their potential customers need than the customers themselves? Why are products deprived of development? Why is professional objectivity abandoned—even if it once might have been possessed? Hell, I don't know the answers.

All I know is that turnarounds do occur and that,

even so, they are far too often mishandled. I may not be able to answer those pesty questions, but I am sure that I can help at least to make some turnarounds more effective. That's why this *Handbook* exists.

So much for the natural history of turnarounds. Before we begin to present the professional approach to achieve the requisite turnaround results (in Section III) let's next describe and define the "successful" turnaround. It's a lot easier to be an expert marksman once we know where the bull's eye is. Following a key principle in *No-Nonsense Planning*, let's carefully identify the end result we want to achieve before we begin trying to obtain it—LAST IS FIRST.

# SECTION II

# WHAT IS A SUCCESSFUL TURNAROUND?

Before we plunge into the "how to" of constructing a tailored turnaround plan, let's invest some time to make sure that we really understand the "what for." Getting *a* turnaround program under way is far less important than getting the *right* turnaround program started. And the only way to make sure that we do have the right remedial program is to understand the nature and characteristics of a "right" program.

Most often a clear understanding of what something *is* can best be grasped by first gaining an understanding of what it *is not*. So, let's begin by discussing why most turnaround programs either fail totally, resulting in the firm going belly-up, or they fail to achieve optimal results.

A turnaround situation is, if it is anything, a time of crisis. The stresses and strains on the entire organization are both new and powerful to the people in the firm. The grapevine is abuzz. Who is "in"? Who's "out"? The versions of what's really happening are as numerous as there are cliques. Everyone is, or should be, concerned about job security. The top brass ought to be concerned because they were the ones who were in place during the gestation period of the crisis.

The middle managers are concerned because they (or some of them at least) saw this coming and fear that they will be caught up in the rush to clean house, to cut costs, and/or to shape up the firm into a lean, mean profit machine.

The hourly ranks are not exempt from anxiety—even if they do belong to a union. Will the firm become bankrupt? What about pensions? Severance pay? Will the firm be closed? Totally? Partially? Will they relocate the plant? And so on.

The lesson? Effective, rational objective decisions and actions are only rarely made or taken during times of crisis. The net result of all of the concern, anxiety, stress, and strain is distraction. The focus on personal survival fractionates the management mentality. Management by "thrashabout" becomes the order of the day! Simple answers are always sought; simplistic actions are usually taken. "Each department must cut expenses by 15 percent [or some other "magic" percentage]." "Reduce payroll by 10 percent in every department." "Stop *all* purchases." "Cancel all company gasoline credit cards." "Cancel all subscriptions to the *Wall Street Journal* for everyone below [a designated organizational level]."

These examples or similar versions of nonsense generated by foolish reactions to crisis have been heard by every reader of this book. Some readers may actually have instituted some of them! Can you imagine? Tsk, tsk.

We're talking about the toll taken by change. This may come as something of a surprise, but turnarounds do *not* cause change! If properly managed, however, they *do* accelerate and telescope the changes that should have been made earlier and in more orderly fashion by alert management. It is the immediacy and intensity of change that can wreak organizational havoc. Generally, the employees, customers, bankers, and vendors all were well aware of your firm's growing malaise. They sensed things were not going well. In many cases, they correctly and specifically identified symptoms and problems. Many were dismayed and frustrated by the seeming prolonged lack of remedial action. Their anxiety grew daily. Then, finally, you were ensconced as the firm's savior. At last. Something will be done!

You will have a relatively short period of time to get things going right again. If you behave professionally, you will be able to avoid the potential stress-related organizational disaster and, instead, will capitalize on the deep desire of employees, customers, bankers, and vendors to see the firm survive, recover, then grow and flourish.

The problem with these "management by thrashabout" decisions and actions is that they will *not* generate, spawn, or result in a successful turnaround. While reducing expenses is always laudable and useful, doing so indiscriminately among all departments or organizational units is worse than being only ineffective. It is actually and profoundly counterproductive. First, it signals the organization that management doesn't really know, comprehensively and specifically, what to do. Second, a uniformly leveled scythe will damage functional performance in some departments because it went too far, and leave waste in other departments because it didn't go far enough.

The latter examples of management by thrashabout only alienate the very group of upper and middle level operational management upon whom the owners must ultimately depend to get their investment healthy again. A degree of alienation is tolerable if the benefit to the firm is significant; that is if, by incurrence, the turnaround will most probably be successful. On the other hand, if the benefit is short of that result, then alienation will only prolong the firm's cure, at best—and preclude it, at worst.

Turnarounds also fail because they are initiated and implemented in the same manner and by the same people who allowed the firm to get into trouble in the first place. Too often, management begins to wield the hammer before they even have a blueprint. Firms never reach a turnaround stage because management spent too much time planning, because they completed plans in too great detail. Investment of management time in planning must never be confused with the paper shuffling done by a management so preoccupied with merely analyzing that they never take decisive action. Firms sometimes do indeed reach turnaround crises because of excessive analyses—it's called paralysis by analysis. The demand for more and more analyses for no purpose other than to have an excuse for making decisions and taking actions (or not), or to build a "protect your fanny" file is an oft-encountered management cop-out. The prevalence of its practice in a firm is usually directly proportional to the number of layers of management and/or the number of people in the respective layers. This type of nonsense must always result in financial trouble, if not financial disaster.

The point to be made here is that the incremental value of time invested in serious planning by far exceeds the incremental value of time invested in "taking action." If the firm is in a turnaround situation, premature action taken by management will produce, at best, suboptimal results because they again place too much emphasis on rushing to take unplanned action—the very same behavior that got them into trouble in the first place.

When you observe this rush to "do something," you can correctly predict failure of the turnaround effort. Because there is only a precious, finite period of time available in which to save the firm, any time spent on either the wrong symptoms or non-severe symptoms will be a complete waste. In other words, turnarounds fail because remedial action taken is not appropriate either to the types of problems that the firm faces or to the severity of those problems. There is only one way to insure that the firm's symptoms are addressed in the effective descending sequence of severity priority. The analytical steps presented in this *Handbook*, if seriously and professionally followed, will provide the data needed for a successful turnaround. While execution of the remedial action is clearly beyond the scope and control of this (or any other) book, at least the owners and creditors will be 99 and 44/100 percent sure of what has to be done.

Another view of why turnarounds fail is that not enough of the "right" action or too much of the "wrong" action was taken. Again, the basic reason for the lack of success can be traced to the absence of a thorough plan that details the action to be taken, the timing and duration of that action, the monitoring and control reporting of progress, and the predetermined, quantitive results expected of the identified action steps.

Earlier, in Section I, you were introduced to the four stages of turnarounds. In reality, there is only *one* stage; namely, insufficient cash and/or cash flow to meet the imminent or future needs of the firm. *But,* there *are* four stages or phases of the cash insufficiency which are distinguished by the imminence of or distance from termination of the firm. A steady or growing positive cash flow is essential not only for the survival of the firm, but also for validity of expectation of any significant internal growth.

While the crucial role of cash flow is indisputable, it is equally indisputable that it can be generated only by a corresponding and antecedent stream of quality profit. The moment that persistent erosion of gross margin content in the forward-aged order backlog begins, the firm requires turnaround treatment. What was identified as Stage 4, Quality of Profit, is really the first stage or phase of a turnaround condition. Most firms enter this phase silently and unnoticed largely because management previously had failed to install a reliable, quantitative early-warning reporting system. The quality of a firm's profit will eventually and inexorably deteriorate if left unattended. Increased competition will develop as more firms seek to share the favorable margins enjoyed by the incumbent firm. Or, management will allow unit costs of labor, material, distribution, production, and/or administration to rise without offsetting unit margin increases. Pre-tax return on sales will display a pattern of erosion. It won't plummet, mind you, it will be gradual.

Once the firm is solidly mired in the quality of profit stage, absent relevant and effective management remedial action, the firm *must* drift (or plunge) into the quantity of profit stage of turnaround, or Stage 3. In general, the speed with which the firm's condition deteriorates from the quality of profit stage to the quantity of profit stage is directly proportional to the lack of speed with which remedial action is taken while the firm was in Stage 4. Envision a whirlpool. The speed of the water in the whirlpool increases geometrically as it moves from its first lazy, almost indiscernible, movement at the outer circular surface perimeter to the bottom-most depth of its vortex. Such is the timing pattern of a firm once caught in the turnaround whirlpool. First, the quality of profit erodes. Usually, unfortunately, soon the quantity of profit also erodes as the firm picks up speed en route to financial oblivion. When the erosion of quantity of profit is sufficient, the firm sinks lower (and even faster) into the cash shortfall stage. If, yet, insufficient effective remedial action is withheld, the firm's financial condition plummets deeper and again even faster into the cash crunch stage. The time interval for effective remedial action is shortened even further and, absent such action, the firm quickly sinks all the way to the vortex and—*it goes down the tubes!*

What is the crucial and useful insight into the nature of turnarounds to be gained from this discussion? Simply stated, a relationship exists between the stage of the severity of the turnaround and the scope, timing, and nature of the remedial action that can (should) be taken. If the alarm is sounded in Stage 4, Quality of Profit, a remedial action program can be formulated free from the debilitating demand to "do" something (for God's sake!) *today*. As with a human patient, the earlier that the symptoms can be correctly diagnosed, the lesser the trauma of the cure, and the more favorable the prognosis.

The earlier the stage that the turnaround symptoms are properly diagnosed, the better the probability of achieving a successful prognosis. The basic reason for the increased likelihood of success is the greater amount of time available with which thoroughly and properly to condition the owners, the creditors, and the operating organization to the changes that are forthcoming as documented in the turnaround action plan. The earlier that the need for changes is brought to the attention of the owners, the creditors, and the operating organization, the more receptive and supportive they will be. As their receptivity and support increases, so too does the likelihood of successful implementation.

Thus, treating the stages or phases of a turnaround as "types" of turnarounds is useful because the nomenclature itself suggests that differing and different management actions are appropriate to each.

Let's move along to discuss what a successful turnaround *is*. A successful turnaround consists of only two elements. First, there must be a turnaround plan. Second, that plan must be published and communicated.

The preparation of the turnaround plan is dealt with in necessary detail in Section VI. Only a preview of the highlights will be presented here. Of towering importance is the realization that the plan *must* be tailored and customized to the particular firm at a particular point in time. There are *no* panaceas. There is no universal solution; there can be no universal plan. Just as each human patient must be individually treated for a successful cure, so too must a corporate patient receive individual treatment. The differences between firms and the variables within the firm at different times are so significant and yet so subtle that more analytical tools, rather than fewer, are needed to distinguish them properly. The objective that is sought by careful and painstaking tailoring is, of course, to produce a documented set of relevant, priority-ranked, measurable, do-able management actions such that, upon successful execution, the enduring value of the owners' investment is enhanced.

By the way, the reason that almost all books dealing with turnaround management fall so far short of providing practical help to the reader is the lack of proper understanding of the necessity for tailoring the plan to the situation, rather than vice versa. For instance, the reader's heart will leap when he reads in a recent "how to" book that a manager's secretary should help him conserve his time. Really! Or that, in a turnaround situation, management should rush to hire a quality control manager, a personnel manager and an MIS (Management Information Systems) manager. Come on! When a firm is in trouble you need to know tactics—not generalized, platitudinous strategies.

Back to the mainstream. Development of the plan is, of course participatory and iterative. Two activities are performed concurrently. One of them deals directly with the owners and/or creditors if we face a cash crunch or cash shortfall. In concert with the owners/creditors, the "target" pro-forma statements are quantified—cash flow, balance sheet, and income statement. "Target" statements are defined as those which display results that meet or exceed the levels required for survival of the firm. Focus should, at least initially, be made on the *minimum* levels of performance that are needed. Of principal importance is the debt service load we face in a cash crunch or cash shortfall turnaround. Return-on-equity performance gains in importance if the firm faces either a quantity or quality of profit situation.

As the target financial statements are being developed, the symptoms are defined and quantified using the appropriate analytical tools. Remedial actions are first inferentially derived from the quantitative symptoms; then, the priority-ranked actions are similarly and conformingly quantified. Cash flow, balance sheet and income statements are then derived from the quantified actions and their validity or do-ability is tested by comparative evaluation to the Three P's and to the sanity checks as listed in *No-Nonsense Planning* (Free Press, 1984). If the derived financials satisfy these two requirements, they are then compared to the target financial statements to insure that the needs and requirements of the owners/creditors are satisfied.

It is important to stress that the remedial actions must be defined in terms of personal accountability and measurability. *How To Measure Managerial Performance* (Macmillan, 1980) provides you with extensive arrays of measurements of job performance for all functions of the firm.

The final point to be made is that the remedial actions must be effective rather than only efficient. That is, they must deal with substantive actions which, if properly executed, will contribute significantly to the target forecast results. They must be relevant and directly responsive to the quantified symptoms. Developing a new product may be a worthwhile effort, but it is irrelevant to the cash crunch symptom of inability to meet payroll. A more thorough distinction between "effective" and "efficient" is made in *No-Nonsense Management* (Macmillan, 1977).

Once the final plan has been documented, the remaining element of turnaround success is communication of the plan. Keeping in mind that survival of the firm ultimately rests with operating management personnel, we see that the need for each employee to understand what is expected of him or her is both obvious and great. One simply cannot perform satisfactorily if one is ignorant of what is expected. Further, the more complete the understanding of the roles that other employees will play, the greater the opportunity to establish meaningful teamwork. Morale of the operating personnel is a crucial consideration. Thus, communication of the plan including interim progress reports to the operating personnel is of crucial importance. Eyeball-to-eyeball contact is most preferable.

If the firm is facing a cash crunch or cash shortfall turnaround stage, special pains must be taken to inform union leadership at local, national, and international levels. Such contact is essential to lay the foundation for successful contract renegotiation if that is required for the firm's survival.

Of course, early communication to the owners and/or creditors is a "must." In addition to communication of the plan itself, the owners/creditors must be informed of the monitoring and control reporting system which will be used to track interim performance to predetermined milestones. The owners and creditors will be persuaded to withhold disinvestment and/or credit call action.

# SECTION III

# SYMPTOMS OF THE TYPE OF TURNAROUND

### Overview

The purpose of this section is to present the twenty-eight symptoms of imminent and/or eventual financial distress of a business firm. The symptoms relate, generally, to manufacturing firms, but many of them can be easily and profitably applied to service or resale firms as well. They are presented generally in sequence of immediacy of financial disaster. Those symptoms usually revelatory of cash crunch are presented first, cash shortfall next, then quantity of profit, and finally quality of profit. Of course, there is some overlap, and in selected cases any symptom may prove useful with respect to more than one turnaround stage or phase.

It is important that you become more than passingly familiar with all of the symptoms. Overlooking one or another of them in your initial examination may lead to incorrect inferences, inappropriate remedial treatment, an unnecessarily prolonged cure, or even demise of the firm. In your first reading, then, carefully pore over each of the twenty-eight. Then, as you face real-world situations, keep this *Handbook* nearby so that you can use it as a reference checklist to make sure that you have touched all of the bases.

There are two cardinal principles related to effective symptom identification and measurement. The first is to "unitize" the measurements. That is, wherever practical and feasible, evaluate the data in terms of *each* unit of product or service. The common sense of this approach is obvious. The firm makes/sells/delivers only one "unit" of a product or service at a time. A great deal of the firm's money is spent in that exact pattern. Making, selling, and delivering "units" are the only ways in which virtually all of the firm's cash inflow is generated. It is impossible to know too much about the firm's "unit" of business behavior.

The second principle is to relate the data concerning unit costs and revenues to product line, customer, channel of distribution, and geographic region. The two perpetual questions asked by the management of any progressive firm are "Where is the money coming from?" and "Where does the money go?" Using unit data as the diagnostic quanta, meaningful tracking of inflow-outflow can be confidently accomplished. There is nothing so devastating to an opinion as a number but there is no more commanding and compelling an opinion than one that is based on arrays of hard, verifiable numbers.

As you proceed through this section, you will be reminded, ad nauseum, of the need to conform incessantly to these two principles.

Remember that what you will read deals *only* with the symptom. The diagnostic and analytical tools used to derive inferences from the symptom data are presented in Section IV. Remedial actions to alleviate the symptoms are presented in Section V. The aim of this section is to position you so that you will be able to *use* the symptoms, first to ascertain the stage of turnaround that you are dealing with, and second to properly select the appropriate remedial action. We are at Step 1 of Figure 1 and what we want to do is determine which financial infirmity is hurting the firm so that only productive treatments will be prescribed. Appendix 5 summarizes, in a practical reference table format, the symptoms which correspond to each major group of actions.

Each symptom is discussed in two parts: the first is the definition of the symptom; the second is the means used to quantify the symptom. Quantification, in turn, consists of *two* elements. First, of course, is the number of dollars, number of units, number of people, and other numbers naturally associated with the symptom. Second, the timing associated with the symptom must be calendarized into the future and backwards into the near past as well. Our aim is to discover *when* the suffering associated with the symptom will become unbearable or fatal.

Many of the definitions and means of quantification will be familiar. Many definitions will be self-evident from the name of the symptom. Do *not* look for "magic wands"—there are *none*. What you should constantly be looking for is the most effective way to *use* the symptom data.

### Symptom 1. Inability to Pay Debt Service

Simply stated, the firm has not generated enough cash and/or is not generating enough cash to pay the interest on outstanding debt when it becomes due. Even if the management does not regularly prepare cash flow forecasts, the banks and other creditors do and will soon bring the situation to the attention of management. Rest assured that one way or another, the symptom *will* surface!

The only reliable method of quantification is the periodic and consistent preparation of cash flow forecasts. Let's go into some detail about the periodicity of cash flow forecast preparation because the principles equally apply to quantification of Symptoms 1 through 7. Also, because cash and cash flow comprise the lifeblood of any firm, too much care and attention cannot be given.

There are four time periods which should consistently be used to monitor the quantity and quality of cash flow. The quality of cash flow is important. For instance, depreciation, which is usually computed on an annual basis, is normally included in cash or funds flow statements—and, of course, it should be. However, it is certainly of lesser quality and value than say, cash generated by an increasing margin on an increasing volume. Besides, its impact is more future than imminent.

The first, and shortest, time period is a three-month "rolling" forecast. You know, add a month and drop a month at the end of each month, *irrespective of fiscal quarters*. Fiscal quarters, and years for that matter, are only accounting system accommodations. The business will grow and thrive, or it will not, neither knowing nor caring which quarter or which year it is in.

The format used in the three-month rolling forecast can be an abbreviated cash flow statement. Pareto's law is alive and well—20 percent or less of the cash-related accounts will bear 80 percent or more of the cash traffic. Thus, a fixed, though abbreviated, format can be effectively used. Dedicate one line on the forecast to "open purchase orders" as a reminder to empty the drawers in the purchasing department of commitments made during the month.

Once a little experience is gained, it will be possible to prepare surprise-free forecasts easily. Familarity with the cash outflow accounts will generate confidence that all spigots of major cash expenditures will have been included. Spend more time to verify the outflows than the inflows! Minor errors of forecast inflows are far more easily and quickly forgiven than are omissions of outflows. Omission of an inflow will only cause you to "fail-up."

Do not waste time or energy by trying to embody excessive precision. The cash flow forecast should be, first and foremost, a management report—not an accounting report. The required accounting reports can be prepared later. It is far more important, i.e., useful, for management to learn that the firm will be short of cash by *about* $100,000 three months from now than it is to learn that the firm will be short of cash by *exactly* $98,743.24 just two days from now. More discussion of approximation in Section IV.

The second time period to be used for cash flow forecasts (and all of Symptoms 1–7, don't forget) is a flexible period. It should include a range of three to nine months depending upon the firm's seasonal effects on cash inflow/outflow. If the rolling three-month forecast is termed "imminent," then this rolling three-to-nine month forecast can be called "short-term." Where the imminent forecast can best reveal "cash crunch" symptoms, the short-term forecast most effectively displays "cash shortfall" symptoms.

The remaining two time periods are more useful for uncovering profit-problem symptoms rather than cash-problem symptoms. A "medium-term" forecast encompasses a six-to-twelve-month time period. A "long-term" forecast normally includes a twelve-month period and is often tied or compared to previously documented three- or five-year business plans.

### Symptom 2. Inability to Pay "Taxes"

Included in this symptom is the firm's inability to pay *all* governmental levies, not only taxes on real estate, personal property, income, and so on. Think too, in terms of municipal and state licenses, and the like.

The quantification of this symptom can be achieved by following the pattern described in Symptom 1. Care must be taken to insure that *all* cognizant governmental units and levels are included in the calendarization. Also, be sure to include payments related to workmen's compensation—they too are a form of taxation.

### Symptom 3. Inability to Pay Contractual Obligations

This category includes post-sale or warranty obligations, royalties, licenses, and so on. While these obligations may represent significant cash outflows in some firms, in others they may not. But, because of the lack of common pay dates, some of these obligations can be (and too often are) overlooked. The best sources of quantification data are the contracts file and the customer file. Don't overlook retainers to law firms, accounting firms, consultants and so on. In many firms, these obligations are recorded on a purchase order and thus should be quantified during the accounts payable examination.

While performing the investigation, also look for and note obligations to reduce product selling price in the future to certain customers as a means of warranty settlement. Be sure to include dividend payment requirements. Quantification can best be achieved by using the four time periods presented above in Symptom 1.

### Symptom 4. Inability to Pay Accounts Payable

Essentially, what we're dealing with here is the situation where vendors have already been stretched beyond even "delayed" or "late" payment. COD requirements probably have already been imposed. Refusals to make further shipments to the firm may already have been given.

When using calendarization to quantify this symptom, be sure to build in a payment stretchout beyond the stated terms. But be sure to calculate the "cost" of discounts lost thereby. We certainly do not want to reduce cash flow unnecessarily or punish profit for the sake of blind adherence to a vendor "stretchout rule."

### Symptom 5. Inability to Pay Salaries, Wages, Commissions

In this case the firm cannot make timely payment of what is commonly called *direct* compensation to employees and/or agents.

During quantification, observe the periodicity of payment of the compensation elements. Evaluate whether changes in payment periods would mitigate the symptom without raising latent operating problems because of opposition to the changes from the recipients. Be mindful that contractual limitations may exist which bar changes. Two examples are union contract provisions relative to pay terms and agency contracts covering either time and/or method of payment.

### Symptom 6. Inability to Pay Fringes, Pensions, Etc.

Where Symptom 5 dealt with *direct* compensation elements, here we deal with *indirect* compensation elements.

Our focus is on timing and amount of payments to insurance firms, pension funds, and the like. Provision should be made for vacation, holiday, and other special "day off" pay. Generally, these elements should amount to no more than some 30–40 percent of the total direct compensation payments. Separate the cash payment requirements from the expense accrual provisions. While pension fund contributions, say, may be accrued monthly, payments may occur only semiannually. The accrual provisions affect only profit, whereas the payment itself will affect only cash flow. The monthly accrual profit impacts are always less than the payment cash impact. Perhaps that may seem a somewhat fatuous statement, but the dissimilarity of impact on the two financial statement forecasts can be quite pronounced and should not be overlooked.

### Symptom 7. Inability to Pay Purchase Commitments

Symptom 4 dealt with debts that are outstanding, due, and owing to vendors. This symptom deals with future delivery of materials and services which will be directly incorporated into the firm's product. This is exemplified where the firm issues a blanket purchase order with scheduled delivery dates.

Another example, which usually has significant impact on cash flow, is scheduled delivery of capital equipment or outsourced prototypes and models.

## Symptom 8. Excessive Debt/Equity Ratio

Simply stated, when the total debt of a firm is divided by the value of the shareholder equity, the resultant ratio expresses this relationship between these two balance sheet items. Taken in isolation, the ratio is of virtually no use to us at all! It may range all the way from less than 1.0 to more than 10.0.

This is the first symptom where the value and common sense of this *Handbook* become eminently apparent. Namely, if the corporate patient told you, the company doctor, that it had a debt/equity ratio of 6.7, you would have no idea whether to be alarmed, indifferent, or elated. The need to combine *this* quantified symptom with others validates and illustrates the approach espoused in this *Handbook;* namely, that effective, relevant turnaround management can only be prescribed after all of the symptoms are quantified so that only accurate and comprehensive diagnostic inferences can be made.

It can summarily be said that *any* debt/equity ratio is excessive if the firm displays Symptom 1 to a pronounced degree or for a prolonged period. Conversely *any* debt/equity ratio is not excessive so long as there is sufficient cash flow to service the debt comfortably, that is, to meet the interest payments and principal repayments "easily" as they become due and owing.

Another often useful measure is the pattern of ratio behavior over time—both the recent past and the meaningful future. You may uncover a portent of financial trouble. But, a great deal more of this when I discuss the diagnostic, analytical tools in Section IV.

## Symptom 9. Flat, Falling Sales

The firm's prior period income statements are used to quantify this symptom. Use the "net" sales line for monthly, quarterly, and annual data. The "gross" sales line is not particularly useful because it fails to exclude returns and allowances and other deductions from revenues. Accounts receivable, the principal source of cash inflow, consists only of net sales. Because cash flow behavior is of paramount interest in a Stage 1, turnaround diagnosis can be erroneous if gross sales data are used.

Similarly, the magnitude of pre-tax potential generated by sales is limited by the amount of net sales. And, since quantity and quality of profit streams are legitimate subjects for turnaround analysis, there is no point at all in injecting cash or profit potential error by use of bloated numbers.

At this stage, we are not yet interested in explanations for the flat, falling sales performance. Our sole concern is to reliably quantify the fact that sales are (or are not) flat or falling. Gathering data by product line, by customer, by distribution channel, and by geographic region will prove of great value later.

Don't invest a lot of time studying volume—volume is nothing! *Margin* is everything!

### Symptom 10. Eroding Gross Margin

The number that we seek to quantify is arrived at by subtracting cost of goods sold from net sales. In some firms this difference is called gross margin. In other firms, it is called standard margin. This latter nomenclature is commonly found when the firm uses (or thinks it uses) a standard cost system of accounting for the measurement of product costs and inventory additions and reliefs.

The source of the data is the firm's prior income statements. Again, as with Symptom 9, classification of gross margin by product line, by customer, by distribution channel, and by geographic region significantly aids later analysis.

### Symptom 11. Increasing Unit Labor Cost

When the cost of labor per unit of product trends consistently upward, gains in productivity are more than offset or negated by increases in compensation—either direct or indirect—paid to labor. Here we are dealing with so-called direct and indirect labor who are utilized to manufacture or otherwise produce the products or services that the firm sells. Conventionally, "direct" labor is that which is incorporated directly into the product or service. There is a "hands-on" relationship.

"Indirect" labor denotes the support and complementary personnel who assist direct labor to position or prepare the product or service for shipment and delivery to the customer. Sometimes, indirect labor includes those personnel who support the product after sale and delivery is completed.

Financially, the distinction between these two groups is that direct labor costs can be charged directly to each unit of product in a relatively consistent and accurate manner. Indirect labor costs, on the other hand, are generally not assignable to each unit of product. These costs are spread over all units of product usually by accumulation in the burden or factory overhead accounts. This type of labor cost is covered in detail in Symptoms 13 through 16 below.

The most useful measure, that is, the one that provides the greatest insight for turnaround analyses, is *hours* of direct labor incurred per unit of product output. Traditionally, *dollars* of cost per unit of product output are used exclusively. The use only of dollars condemns the company doctor to view the real condition of the firm only dimly, through a glass darkly. A moment's thought reveals why this is so.

Dollars are affected by the hourly rate paid to direct labor. Thus, the dollars per unit ratio must always rise, given no change in productivity of direct labor.

Data may be garnered from account cost records, operational records, attendance records, shipping records, invoices, inventory withdrawal records, and so on. Yet again, measurement by product line, by customer, by distribution channel, and by geographic region significantly enhances the likelihood of precision of remedial treatment.

### Symptom 12. Increasing Unit Material Cost

What we are quantifying is the cost of material incorporated in each unit of product. Again, there are direct materials and indirect materials. The distinction is closely akin to that used to distinguish direct and indirect labor. Direct material is incorporated directly into the product unit itself. Indirect material, such as shipping cartons, shipping supplies, and so on cannot easily be traced to each discrete unit. Usually, the accounting cost incurred in the attempt to trace these costs greatly outweighs the value of the resultant cost accounting. Indirect material costs are usually accumulated in factory burden or overhead accounts for distribution among all products.

Only rarely is it the case that unit material costs increase because more physical material is used or consumed. Almost without exception, you will find that unit material costs have risen because prices paid for that material have increased more than any savings that may have been captured by reduction in purchase costs, cost of purchasing, or material substitution.

Cost accounting records, receiving reports, and accounts payable records are among the potential sources for data quantification. Classification by product line, by customer, by channel of distribution, and by geographic region can bolster analytical capability.

## INCREASING UNIT BURDEN EXPENSE

The relationship between Symptoms 13, 14, 15, and 16 is illustrated in Figure 2.

|  | PEOPLE-RELATED | PLANT-RELATED* |
|---|---|---|
| CONTROLLABLE OR VARIABLE | *Symptom 13*<br>Payroll, "fringes," travel, education, overtime premium, etc. | *Symptom 15*<br>Supplies, maintenance, utilities, tools, etc. |
| NON-CONTROLLABLE OR FIXED | *Symptom 14*<br>Payroll, "fringes," travel, education, overtime premium, etc. | *Symptom 16*<br>Taxes, insurance, statutes, regulations, equipment, etc. |

*Very often, product-related costs are included in this category. See Symptoms 11 and 12.

**Figure 2.** Burden Expense Symptom Anatomy

Before proceeding to discuss each of the four symptoms, let's explain the labels on the rows and columns. The rows are separated into the two traditional categories: controllable or variable, and noncontrollable or fixed. Variable costs are always fixed or constant *per unit* of product/service, whereas fixed costs always vary *per unit* of product/service. This cost behavior underlines the need, again, for expressing symptomatic data in unit terms.

Because variable costs are fixed per unit, the total variable costs will rise or fall with changing levels of operation. Conversely, the so-called fixed costs, which, in total, remain unchanging during the fiscal period, will be spread among more or fewer units as operational levels fluctuate.

Another distinction centers on the length of time needed to make a significant change in cost/expense run-rates. There is, of course, no such thing as a completely noncontrollable or fixed cost. *ALL* costs/expenses are ultimately controllable or variable. But some expenses naturally tend to rise and fall as production volume varies. The costs of direct material and direct labor are examples. Of course, no expense will fall by itself. Expenses tend to rise by inflation. But expenses can be reduced *only* by decisive management action.

To clarify the distinction further, consider the notion of reversibility/irreversibility. Firing a material handler, for example, can be relatively easily, quickly, and inexpensively reversed. Whereas closing a plant or warehouse, or disposing of capital equipment are examples, realistically speaking, of irreversible actions. Thus, while there is considerable gray area between controllable and noncontrollable, the easier and cheaper it is to remove and restore the cost/expense element, the more it resembles a controllable item. And vice versa.

The columns are divided into the two principal components of burden or overhead expense—people and plant. A third, but usually less significant component is product, that is, those costs related to particular products or product lines. This product-related component is discussed separately in Symptom 12. In brief, it is usually the case that the lion's share of burden expense is related to, caused, or generated by, either people or the plant (facilities) itself.

### Symptom 13. Increasing Burden: People-Related Variable Expense

These are the costs that are usually associated with keeping personnel on the payroll. Further, these people usually are employed in production "support" roles, such as material handler or forklift operator.

Personnel records, operational rosters, payroll records, union contracts (particularly those provisions dealing with job classifications), and accounting statements are among the sources of quantification data.

### Symptom 14. Increasing Burden: People-Related Fixed Expenses

The nature of these costs and the quantification data sources are essentially the same as those described in Symptom 13. The difference between the two symptoms is the type of job performed by the personnel under review. Namely, the people under consideration in this symptom are even more remote from actual product manufacture than those personnel included in Symptom 13. Their jobs are less "hands-on" even than those included in Symptom 13.

Some examples of personnel in this symptom include department foreman (foreperson), industrial engineer, purchasing agent, and, in general, operational supervisory and management personnel.

### Symptom 15. Increasing Burden: Plant-Related Variable Expense

These are expenses that (*should*) vary with the level of production. Supplies and tools, for example, which are used up, consumed, or worn out by the production processes or activities are included in this category. So, too, are utilities such as water and electricity that are utilized in the production process. Even plant maintenance expenses should vary (at least somewhat) with varying levels of production.

Expense ledgers, accounts payable, inventory records, and work orders are four examples of quantification data sources.

### Symptom 16. Increasing Burden: Plant-Related Fixed Expense

Similar to the distinction mentioned earlier between Symptoms 13 and 14, the expenses included in this category are more remote from the actual production process than those included in Symptom 15. In this category, for example, there are expenses such as taxes, insurance, and payments that are mandatory because of the need to comply with statutes, ordinances, or regulations.

In addition to the data sources identified in Symptom 15, you will find contract files and legal files to be of help. Usually, in an ongoing business, the basic accounting records will (or at least should) suffice.

## Symptom 17. Increasing Sales/Marketing Expense

Even if population levels stay the same, sales/marketing expenses have a propensity to increase steadily year after year because of salary and wage increases, and because of the effect of inflation on the cost of supplies, travel, and other purchased materials or services.

The basic accounting system expense records should suffice to provide means to quantify the data. Be alert to the possibility of lack of comparability between prior periods because of changes in accounting system classifications.

What we are trying to quantify are the costs and expenses incurred in the firm's efforts to promote and obtain the sale of its products/services. These include people-related costs and expenses: salaries, wages, commissions, "fringes," and so on. Also, expenses are incurred for purchased materials and services, including market research reports, advertising campaigns, consultants' fees, promotion programs, and so on.

## Symptom 18. Increasing Finance/Administration Expense

Aside from (but in addition to) the conventional expenses—that is, those related to personnel and office facilities—the behavior of interest expense should receive special, highlighted attention. This is a crucial number because of its relationship to the ability of the firm to meet its debt service obligations.

Comments about quantification data sources in Symptom 17 apply equally here.

## INCREASING ENGINEERING EXPENSE

The relationship between these Symptoms 19, 20, 21, and 22 is illustrated in Figure 3.

Engineering expense is very often a many-faceted phenomenon; sometimes it is even a many splendored thing. It is sometimes a blend, but usually you will find that it is only a mixture of expenses. And, if the firm really is in a turnaround mode, even the ingredients of the mixture will not be clearly differentiated. But then again,

|  | PEOPLE-RELATED | PRODUCT-RELATED |
|---|---|---|
| IN-HOUSE | *Symptom 19*<br>Payroll, wages, salaries, fringes, travel, entertainment, training, education, etc. | *Symptom 21*<br>Supplies, models, equipment, test instruments, test laboratory, etc. |
| CONTRACT | *Symptom 20*<br>Hourly or other period fees and charges, travel, etc. | *Symptom 22*<br>Progress payments, models, samples, prototypes, interim developments, etc. |

**Figure 3.** Engineering Expense Symptom Anatomy

your job as the company doctor is to sort it all out, isn't it?

There are all sorts of "engineering" expenses. They include industrial engineering, manufacturing engineering, design engineering, development engineering, sales engineering, quality engineering, research engineering, material engineering, cost reduction engineering, and other shades and variations of these. But, through it all, there are only two ways in which engineering expenses can be incurred. You either hire engineers (technicians and support personnel are also included in this discussion) and put them on the payroll (so-called in-house), or you "buy" engineering expertise from another firm with whom you enter into a "contract." What we have done thus far is describe the classification of the rows of Figure 3.

With regard to the columns in Figure 3, engineering expenses stem from two principal sources—people and product. Of course, there are occasions when engineering expense is related to plant, the third of the Three P's. But generally, once the business is ongoing, the amount of expense devoted to plant is (and should be) only a small proportion of the amounts spent on people and product. Further, it is rare indeed that a turnaround situation is precipitated by uncontrolled expenses related to plant.

**Symptom 19. Increasing Engineering In-House People-Related Expense**

The nature of these expenses is identical to the nature of the expenses in Symptoms 13 and 14. They are incurred as a direct result of having people on the payroll. Recall that putting someone on the payroll generates far more expense than only the compensation paid to that individual. And this is even more true of engineering personnel than those in other functions. To keep up with the "state of the art," training, seminars, conventions, books, periodicals, and so on can become as expensive as the compensation paid, and sometimes even more so.

This symptom can be quantified, by and large, from the same data sources used with Symptoms 13 and 14.

### Symptom 20. Increasing Engineering Contract People-Related Expense

Essentially, these expenses are fees paid to another firm for the professional, technical services of their personnel. Note that the "fringes" are almost always excluded. Whether the fees are levied on an hourly basis or according to some other time period is controlled by the provisions of the contract between the two firms.

The most reliable data source for quantification is the contract itself. Supporting accounting records, especially accounts payable, are also a useful source.

### Symptom 21. Increasing Engineering In-House Product-Related Expense

These expenses, largely, are incurred to acquire either materials or routine services (e.g., testing) pursuant to completion of a product-related project. All professionally managed engineering functions are planned, monitored, and controlled by project authorization techniques and reporting systems. Therefore, project records, if properly maintained, will provide quantification data for materials drawn from inventory and for purchases of supplies, equipment, and so on.

Unfortunately, if the firm is indeed in a turnaround situation, the availability of these records will most probably be slight to nil. Therefore, most of the time you will have to reconstruct data from records both within and outside of the accounting system.

### Symptom 22. Increasing Engineering Contract Product-Related Expense

In almost all cases the contract with the outside firm stipulates all payments associated with prototypes, models, preproduction units, breadboards, and so on. Also, any progress payments and the trigger conditions under which they become due and owing are also usually embodied in the contract. The preferred data source for quantification, then, is the contract, augmented by supporting accounting records data.

Caveat: Take special steps to insure that the contract file is current. That is, verify that any and all modifications and/or change orders have been (1) properly and conformingly executed and (2) included in the contract file. Measure carefully your *legal* obligations. In a turnaround situation where the survival of the firm is at stake, disregard all considerations other than the enforceable legal obligations of all parties. Hold the other parties rigorously to their obligations and honor only those which are inescapable. Too often it is the case that, if a firm is in a turnaround, contract administration has been performed in something less than an effective and efficient manner.

### Symptom 23. Inconsistent Valuation of Inventory Input/Output

Unbelievable though it may seem, there are many, many instances where profits have been distorted because production costs are valued differently from cost of production. Labor, material, and burden costs are incurred as production activity proceeds and are charged to inventory. When the finished product is sold, the cost of that production is subtracted from the sales price to determine gross margin. It is also subtracted from inventory.

Thus labor and material reporting systems can (and do, if imperfectly maintained and administered) seriously affect the accuracy of reported period profits. Of particular importance is the floor reporting system of labor costs. Labor costs are usually measured by time-card reporting to work orders, and usually amount to some 10–20 percent of total production cost. So, if labor hours are unreported, or if they are improperly valuated, the value of the input to inventory will be correspondingly affected.

But, more important is the "multiplier effect" of burden costs. Generally, burden cost is "absorbed" on a percentage basis of each labor hour or dollar expended. For example, if burden costs for the year are budgeted or estimated to be $100, and labor cost is budgeted or estimated to be $50, then a burden rate of absorption of 200 percent is derived by dividing the burden cost by the labor cost. As labor cost dollars are incurred, they are multiplied by the 200 percent rate of absorption to compute the associated burden cost that will be charged to inventory. Thus, *every* erroneous labor dollar really affects inventory input by *three* dollars!

Usually, this discrepancy is detected and corrected when physical inventory is taken. The adjustment can occur only in one of two ways. If inventory output, i.e., cost of goods sold, has been consistently *understated*, profits to that same extent have been *overstated*. The inventory shown on the books of account will be greater than that determined by the physical inventory. The reconciliation, or "write-down," is called an inventory "bust" and the difference between the two numbers is deducted from profits.

The converse is true. When cost of goods sold, or inventory relief, has been consistently *overstated*, then profits have been *understated* to that extent, inventory on the books of account has been understated, and the book-to-physical reconciliation will result in (1) a write-up of book inventory and (2) an increase in reported profits. While a write-up *is* better than a write-down, all significant variations or surprises are anathema to professional management because they are symptomatic of a lack of control which, in turn, casts clouds on credibility with owners and creditors.

Quantification data sources include prior audits and

audit reports ("blue-backs"), internal audit records, historical inventory valuation reconciliations, labor reporting systems, receiving records, and so on.

### Symptom 24. Increasing Warranty Expense

Warranty expenses are incurred after the sale and delivery of the product have been completed. Despite exhaustive best efforts, no firm ever consistently delivers "zero-defect" products or services. Thus, incurrence of warranty expense is a normal business expense. Some is good, too much *is* too much.

Warranty expense should vary proportionally to the engineering content in the product. That is, the more technical or complex the product, the higher is the acceptable rate of warranty expense.

Warranty expense can, and almost always does, consist of both labor and material ingredients. Service/repair personnel exemplify the typical people-related cost. Replacement of product, either wholly or partially, exemplifies material-related cost.

The most fruitful sources of data quantification are warranty/service expense records maintained by product or product-line by customer, by channel of distribution and by geographic region.

### Symptom 25. Decreasing Capacity Utilization

As capacity utilization drops, unabsorbed burden expense rises. It's as simple as that. There is the presumption that realistic capacity measurements have been calculated for the plant as a whole, and preferably also for each operating department.

Accounting system records are *not* the best source of quantification data because capacity is expressed best (i.e., most usefully) in terms of physical units—pieces, pounds, gallons, etc. Therefore reliance on operating records such as work orders, shipping documents, and so on, is mandatory.

Relating capacity utilization measures wherever possible to products or product lines dramatically enhances the diagnostic value of this symptom also.

**Symptom 26. Decreasing Product Line Profitability**

Only infrequently, if not rarely, will you find these data to be readily available. What you should be looking for is some form of measurable product line profit performance. Probably the most useful form of product line profitability is calculated by subtracting the associated sales/marketing product line expense from the corresponding gross margin for the same product line. Also, further subtracting warranty expense for that product line supplies a very useful refinement, especially when the product has a relatively high engineering content because warranty expense will then tend to be significant.

The source of these data is the accounting system. But, bear in mind that *all* revenues, costs, and expenses are subject to judgmental and stylistic treatment, as we all know. While differences of accounting treatment may occur, so long as the methods and techniques of accounting treatment are consistent for historical periods under review, the inferences drawn from the data will seldom suffer from gross error.

### Symptom 27. Decreasing Unit Sales

A type of "acid test" can be crossruffed against Symptom 26. Suspicious as we always should be of data obtained from the accounting system, tracing unit sales brings reality to the examination of our corporate patient. Such is the stuff of which unit sales data is composed.

The sources of quantification data include shipping documents in addition to invoice data.

### Symptom 28. Decreasing Customer Profitability

One of the most frequently used arguments for retention of an unprofitable product line is that it is required in order to retain this or that customer. Sometimes the argument is valid. Usually it is not.

This symptom is calculated by accumulating costs as well as sales by customer. Once product, sales/marketing, and warranty costs and expenses are subtracted from revenues, the profitability by customer can be calculated. Do *not* expect these data to be available at the outset. If they were, you most probably wouldn't be called upon to cure the firm.

Be mindful that virtually all of the quantification data

must come from the accounting system. Again, consistency of accounting system judgments and compromises is most important—and in fact is more useful than the rationale used to make those judgments and compromises.

# SECTION IV

# DIAGNOSTIC, ANALYTICAL TOOLS

### Overview

The most cogent and penetrating insight available in this entire galaxy that I can give to you is this: if the *only* tool you have is a hammer, you will view every problem only as a nail! I want to make sure that you will always have more than only a hammer in your management tool kit as you face the complex challenge of a turnaround.

This section arms you with both macro-tools and micro-tools. Macro-tools are those which either (1) blend the data from several symptoms/remedies or (2) can be used to assess and evaluate more than a single symptom/remedy. The former tools are combinative in function whereas the latter tools are more of a "general purpose" type.

The nature of each of the two classes of tools underlines the imperative for the symptoms/remedies to be expressed in as small and discrete a meaningful unit as possible.

They provide the building blocks with which the diagnosis can be successfully constructed. The effectiveness of the synthethis is totally dependent upon the thoroughness of the antecedent anatomization.

The purpose and use of these tools are, essentially, twofold. First, when applied to symptoms, they provide measurable insight into the severity, intensity, pervasiveness, regularity (or lack of it), and other characteristics of them. Once these parameters have been numerically described, the stage is set for making meaningful management inferences concerning the nature, scope, and type of financial ill that affects the firm—we will be able to determine which stage of turnaround the firm is in. More simply stated, these tools provide the means to assess and rank the symptoms in terms of their impact, singly and in combination, on the firm. The assessment and ranking, in turn, provide the means for a thorough, complete diagnosis.

When applied to quantitative remedial actions, these tools will verify the efficacy of the proposed action. You will be able to confirm that the remedial actions that you have prescribed are indeed responsive to the firm's ills. You will insure that enough action is proposed on the one hand, and that you're not throwing out the baby with the bathwater, on the other hand.

Earlier in this *Handbook,* I referred to Pareto's law to illustrate relationships between sets of data. In this section, particularly, I will make repeated reference to Pareto's law. In the almost inconceivable case that you're unfamiliar with it, let's briefly explain what it's all about.

In essence, what Pareto's law tells us is that, in any

business activity, only 20 percent of the actors generate 80 percent of the action. For example, if we're talking about total company sales, Pareto's law holds that 20 percent of the customers will consistently generate 80 percent of the sales. If we're talking about unit material cost, then we're told that 20 percent of the parts account for 80 percent of the total unit material cost. Or, 20 percent of the firm's vendors account for 80 percent of the firm's purchases. And so on.

Of course the figures 20 and 80 are only rules of thumb. The truly important concept underlying Pareto's law is *not* that it aspires to precision. Rather, it rivets our attention to the relatively few causes or generators of business action. It makes us look at what's going on where the action is. And, that is precisely where management's attention *must* be focused if there is going to be any reasonable probability of achieving acceptable results.

To me, the vital function that Pareto's law serves is to dramatize succinctly the crucial difference between "effective" and "efficient." The effective manager doesn't waste a dime or a minute trying to reduce the manufacturing cost of a product that accounts for only 0.00003 percent of the company's total unit sales. On the other hand, the merely efficient manager will try to make a career out of it!

So, if you are not already a devotee, *now* is the time to become intimately familiar with Pareto's law. I wish that I had thought of it first! Make it second nature in your managerial behavior. I'll try to help you do it with the numerous references to it that you will find in this *Handbook.*

Finally, the prime role of all of these tools is to raise far more questions than they provide answers. But they *will* generate useful, relevant questions. As you obtain the answers, your understanding of the firm's situation will become more and complete. And, of course, as your knowledge and understanding grow, so does the probability that you will select the "right" remedial actions and lead the firm to a successful recovery.

## MACRO-TOOLS

### M1. Financial Statements

The basic financial statements—balance sheet, income statement, and funds (cash) flow—are broad gauge tools at best. If consistently prepared, however, they can provide a track record of important data.

Performing period-to-period comparisons, and perhaps even graphing or charting the comparisons, will reveal the patterns of past financial behavior. Such analyses are of great value when preparing run-rate forecasts. A run-rate forecast projects past and present performance into the future—near term and never more than twelve months. The underlying assumption of such a forecast is that none of the major operating functions will vary significantly, if at all, from the way they behaved in the recent past. The data are merely extrapolated, without disproportionately changing sales volumes, costs, expenses, and so on, *except* for those instances where known and unavoidable circumstances will prevail. This forecast aims to supply you with the resultant financial statements if you opt for the "do nothing new" alternative.

Of course, realism should be injected wherever possible. If you know that a particularly large order will soon be booked (or cancelled), for instance, be sure to include the effect. The same is obviously true for any known impact of significance on any item on any of the financial statements. This run-rate forecast is merely step one in developing *the* turnaround plan as we shall later see.

When dealing with the financial statements, be aware of a serious caveat. The conventional wisdom is that the cash flow statement is the premier statement. It has been held that cash flow is a sort of "acid test" of the validity and legitimacy of the reported earnings of the firm. The notion is that while reported earnings may be subject to vagaries of judgment, interpretation, and just plain accounting "cooking", the truth will out on the cash flow statement, don't you know?

Well, it ain't necessarily so! As reported in the *Wall Street Journal,* C. Casey of Dartmouth and N. Bartczak of Harvard completed a study on the predictive capability of cash flow behavior. Their principal conclusions were that (1) cash flow data, alone, failed to distinguish between healthy firms and those that went belly-up; and (2) cash flow behavior alone was inferior, as a predictor, to a number of less highly touted tools including the more mundane debt/equity and profitability ratios. Remember what I said earlier about having only a hammer in your tool kit? Don't rely too much on any one of the forty-eight tools presented in this section.

## M2. The Art of Approximation

Turnaround management is still, after all, management. It is not bookkeeping, it is not even accounting—it is management. As such, the pursuit of too much precision is not only wasted effort, it will lead you in the wrong direction. Too much precision will clearly identify a particular spruce for you, but it sure as hell won't tell you what the forest is all about. In short, excessive precision results in misfocus of attention.

If the firm is in turnaround trouble, the sooner that it is extricated from it, the better. The firm will *not* recover by itself. Time is at more of a premium, if that's possible, than if the firm were healthy.

Adding precision to data takes time. Adding a great deal of precision takes disproportionately more time. Mindful that the turnaround exercise *is* management, not accounting, the incremental value of added precision is not only not very positive, it is negative because it wastes valuable time.

An example may be useful. When walking through a manufacturing plant for the first time, pace the distance between two support columns. That will tell you *about* how many square feet per bay. Then count the bays. Simple multiplication will then tell you *about* how many square feet are in the plant and *about* how many are devoted to warehousing, actual production, and so on. A good rule of thumb is that if the product has *about* average technological content, the plant should generate *about* $40 to $50 in sales revenue per square foot. So, one more rounded-off mental multiplication will tell you *about* what the sales revenues of the firm are, or should be.

Additional inferences can come more rapidly. With *about* average gross margins of 20–30 percent, the operating pre-tax will be *about* 10–20 percent after deducting "below the line" expenses of *about* 10–20 percent, and so on. A quick cross-check helps accuracy. An average of *about* $30,000 to $40,000 sales per employee is a good benchmark to start with. So, divide the estimated sales by 30,000 and 40,000 and you will know *about* how many employees are or should be employed by the firm.

In the space, literally, of minutes, the practised eye (and brain) can sketch out the current financial statements, particularly the working capital assets. Inventory levels can be *approximated* by coupling an estimate of *about* how many times inventory turns and the number of square feet allocated to inventory. The same insight can be gained about receivables if you use *about* 40–50 days sales outstanding. With these two critical working capital items in place, it will be possible, in many, many instances, to quickly infer *about* what the cash flow situation is.

Further, gauging the work pace in the plant enables you to infer *about* what rate that labor efficiency really is. And, the same applies to direct labor as to indirect labor—and, even office personnel. In other words, even an educated estimate of the work pace of the organization will lead you to additional useful, sometimes critical, inferences.

I'm sure that George Custer would much have preferred to know that there were a "helluva lot" of Sioux warriors waiting for him while he was twenty miles away from the Little Big Horn, than to learn that there were exactly 11,272 braves who would overrun his 231 troopers in precisely 1.267 minutes!!

What you eventually want to define are "unshakeable" facts. But, "unshakeableness" is *not* a function of the number of decimals to which the quantitative fact is carried. If the forearm has a compound fracture, it doesn't really help the doctor at all to know that the protrusion is 1.285 millimeters rather than 3.145 millimeters! Knowing whether it is a "simple" fracture rather than a "compound" fracture is enough of a start for the professional practitioner.

*About* $3 million sales; *about* $300,000 pre-tax profit; *about* $1 million inventory; *about* $400,000 accounts receivable; and so on, *should* be enough of a start for you!

Approximation should not, of course, be carried too far or misused. Approximation is most productive in the diagnostic stage. It allows relatively quick familiarity with the essentials of the situation. It can be useful during formulation of the turnaround plan, but only in a more limited sense. It is not unusual, and often it is preferred, to base financial projections on three premises: optimistic, pessimistic, and most likely. Thus, the eventual performance is projected to be bracketed by at least two parameters. The results, actually, will be *about* those shown as most likely.

The art of approximation can also be effectively utilized when formulating remedial action. Seeking to obtain too precise a result from action taken is a common management failure. Managers too often forget that we live, and do business in, only a 95 percent world. Seeking to extract the very last dollar from the market is a common source not only of frustration but of termination as well.

It has been said many (too many) times that, "Half a loaf is better than none." In a turnaround situation, half a loaf is really *not* better than none. Half a loaf will only prolong the firm's agony of demise. But, on the other hand, 95 percent of a loaf can, and often does, spell the difference between survival and oblivion.

The economic utility of time cannot be overlooked. In other words, it is far better for the owners and creditors to receive only 90 percent of their demands *quickly* than to receive 95 percent or even 100 percent much, much later. The lesson? Simply this. Always choose remedial actions which will *assure* capture of 95 percent of the owner/creditor demands because execution will always be less than perfect.

Don't waste your time or anyone else's trying to *assure* the 99th percent! First, it just won't happen that way; second, the owners and creditors simply won't wait that long before they pull the plug!

As for misuse, the most frequently found practice is that of vague or ambiguous recovery goal/objective definition. Far too often, we find that the individuals in the operating organization are (merely) admonished to, "Do better," "Cut costs," "Reduce inventory," "Work harder," and so on. They are urged only to perform functions, somehow; they are not aiming at objectives or goals. Misuse of approximation in this manner precludes the possibility of holding individuals accountable for their individual performance. More important, this misuse also precludes any rational basis for rewarding outstanding performance. This misuse of approximation obliterates both the stick and the carrot! Operating management has been disarmed. Failure is thus assured. Much more detailed discussion of successful mobilization of the operating organization is found in Section VI.

### M3. The Turnaround Plan

In Section II, we looked at a few key highlights of the structure and nature of the turnaround plan. Here, we will penetrate a little further into the essentials of the turnaround plan.

The Turnaround Plan embodies the junction and confluence of your diagnostic and prognostic efforts. The better the diagnostic job that you did in terms of identification, quantification, and interpretation of the symptoms, the more likely it is that the remedial treatment, given reasonably effective implementation, will be nothing short of successful.

Fortunately, for the corporate general practitioner, the confluence of the two efforts *is* separable. While the analytical and synthetical elements of turnaround management do blend in the turnaround plan, they nevertheless retain their discrete uniqueness.

The Turnaround Plan consists of only three sections or sets of financial exhibits. The common language of all three is the traditional set of financial statements and their respective supporting schedules. First, the income statement can be abbreviated for ease of later mathematical operation. The balance sheet, also, can be abbreviated to focus on working capital (essentially inventories and accounts receivable) and debt service loads, both current (accounts payable) and long-term (mortgages, lines of credit). Finally, derived from the income statement and balance sheet data behavior, is the cash flow statement. The *one* common trait is that all of the financials deal exclusively with the future.

Now, as to the sections. The first set of financial exhibits reflects only the extrapolation of results if management does *nothing* of significance differently. The recent past run-rates are projected into the next twelve months. The data are derived from all of the prior symptom analysis and evaluation after application of the macro- and micro-tools. The exhibits are derived *internally*. That is, oversimplifying, all you do is extend into the future the track record of the recent, relevant past. This set of financial exhibits answers the question, "What would most likely happen if we do nothing new at all?"

The second set of financial exhibits, or the second section, is prepared almost totally from data and sources *external* to the firm. This set of financial exhibits can be prepared concurrently with the first set. Let's call this second set the "target" forecast, while we call the first set the "run-rate" forecast. The target forecast reflects the results which have been identified by the owners/creditors as minimally acceptable. We seek to answer the question, "What are the performance levels that must be achieved to persuade the owners/creditors to withhold disinvestment or credit call action?" Numerous meetings and prolonged negotiations are very often the order of the day. A direct, candid, and frank approach is the only one that should be pursued. Owners and creditors may be taken aback initially by such a no-nonsense approach. Most often, they will not be prepared to answer that question promptly, completely, and realistically. They will need your help, too, to formulate and quantify the answers. Usually, you will find that the sequence in which the three financials is prepared is somewhat reverse to that used to complete the run-rate forecast. Namely, the cash flow statement is usually prepared first because most creditors are vitally interested in learning when (i.e., how soon) they will receive interest and principal repayment. The income statement is next formulated to define the performance required to generate the cash. The balance sheet is finalized last although examinations of inventory and accounts receivable are usually done early on to see if there are opportunities for quick cash.

With these two forecasts in place, the third and final set of financial exhibits is calculated largely by subtraction of the run-rate forecast from the target forecast. The third set of financial exhibits represents, then, the changes in performance which must be accomplished in order for the turnaround to be successful. These financials form a bridge from "do nothing" to "what it takes to be successful." Let's call this third set of financials the "objective" forecast. These statements really display the cumulative result of management's planned remedial actions.

The core of this *Handbook* has been reached! Symptoms lead you to the run-rate forecast. The owners/creditors tell you what the target forecast must look like. And, the difference between those two forecasts is the objective forecast which prognosticates the effect of remedial, restorative action.

## M4. Sanity Checks

Sanity checks are most useful and effective when applied to the planned remedial actions. They help you to insure that the planned action, while bold, aggressive, and challenging, does not violate the underlying operational relationships of the firm. If your corporate patient has been in the nuts-and-bolts business, for instance, it is worse than wishful thinking to prescribe a bootstrap development into bioengineering as a near-term turnaround cure. Most of the sanity checks deal with somewhat more subtle relationships, however. Prudent use of them will answer the question, "Does the prescribed remedial action make sense for this firm at this time?" They are summarized here from *No-Nonsense Planning* (Free Press, 1984) where they are presented with full detailed discussion. In short, use these checks (and any others that you may know of) to test the validity and reality of the action you plan to take:

1. The use of stocking distributors is inversely proportional to the engineering content in the product
2. Cost reduction potential is inversely related to engineering content in the product
3. Cost reduction potential is directly proportional to quantity of product units sold

4. Investment in finished good inventory is inversely related to engineering content in the product
5. Retraining difficulty of personnel is directly related to tenure
6. The degree of management effectiveness is inversely proportional to span of control
7. A little personnel turnover helps (the firm's) profitability; a lot hurts
8. Too much bad debt expense hurts profitability; but so does too little

### M5. Subaccount Analysis

After you have completed the 80/20 analysis, you know which relatively few accounts bear most of the traffic. The typical accounting-type report is prepared by listing the accounts in account and subaccount number sequence. You will *always* be better off if you abandon that report format and use a management report format instead.

The first step is to disregard all account and subaccounts which fail to materially affect the respective functional total. Don't bother with the 80 percent (or more) of the accounts and subaccounts that fail to track activity of less than 20 percent of the firm's dollars.

The most effective way to accomplish this is to have a report prepared consisting of subaccounts (or the smallest unit of accounting to which amounts are posted at all) in descending sequence of *dollar amount* of account balance. The account balance should reflect at least six months of activity before it is excluded from consideration. This will allow enough time to obtain a realistic assessment of account traffic. With the report in front of you, quickly scan the list and draw a line at the amount below which you will not further use or scrutinize. In short, don't bother with small amount, low activity accounts and subaccounts.

It is the relatively big amount and high activity accounts that got the firm into trouble; and it is the behavior changes in precisely those same accounts and subaccounts that will get the firm out of trouble. In brief, this tool can be applied productively to validate and eliminate both symptoms and remedial actions.

## M6. Pre-Tax Return on Sales

This tool is calculated by dividing pre-tax profit by net sales. It must be included in preparation of all forecasts in the turnaround plan: run-rate, target, *and* objective.

Comparison of the run-rate ratio to the objective ratio quickly reveals the magnitude of the challenge facing management. The objective ratio will, of course, always be higher than the run-rate. At issue is the amount by which the run-rate ratio is exceeded by the objective ratio. Is it realistic? Can it be done?

During a twelve-month interval, both increased sales (of presumably profitable products—see Symptom 26), and improved pre-tax from cost reduction (see Symptoms 11 through 16) and expense reduction (see Symptoms

17 through 22) will be needed to register a significant improvement in pre-tax return on sales.

## M7. Pre-Tax Return on Assets

The value of this ratio is determined by dividing operating pre-tax by total assets related to that reported operating pre-tax. This tool, as also with Tools M6 and M8, should be applied to all three forecasts in the turnaround plan: run-rate, target, and objective.

Again, comparing the ratio values for run-rate and objective clearly measures the goal that operating management must hit in order to satisfy the owner/creditor demands as expressed in the target forecast. Also again, the objective forecast ratio will always be higher than the run-rate forecast ratio. The only issue is how to achieve the higher ratio; how to properly prescribe remedial action and motivate the operating management to execute.

There are two and only two ways in which the objective ratio can be achieved. Both can proceed concurrently. The first way is to improve operating pre-tax, following the symptom pattern identified in Tool M6 above.

The second is to reduce the denominator, reduce the assets. Aside from irreversible decisions such as sale or closing of plant and facilities, working capital offers the most promising opportunities in a twelve-month period. But these seeming opportunities must be viewed scrupulously. Inventory reduction, for example, may take the form of offering product to customers on a "fire-sale" price, say, at book value. While it may indeed be possible thereby to reduce inventory asset investment in the short term, the most likely consequence is that such action will preclude future sales of product at presumably higher or profitable margins to the very same customers. In short, be more than a little reluctant to reduce asset investment quickly. At best, it's only a temporary improvement whereas improvement of the operating profit stream represents a far more enduring financial improvement. Much more of remedial action theory and practice in Section V.

## M8. Pre-Tax Return On Equity

Equity is also known as shareholders equity, net worth, book value, and so on. The ratio is calculated by dividing operating pre-tax by the amount of equity shown on the balance sheet, normally the difference between the total assets and total liabilities. Subtracting the run-rate ratio from the target ratio defines the task facing operating management; the difference between the two ratios becomes the objective that operating management must achieve.

Improvement of the ratio by reduction of equity is almost never palatable nor practical. Improvement of operating pre-tax is really the *only* viable action; see discussion in Tool M6 above.

M9.  Profitability of Marketing/Sales Channels

M10.  Profitability of Marketing/Sales Region

M11.  Profitability of Marketing/Sales Representative

These three tools are discussed jointly because of their strong similarity and the commonality of their computation. A combination of symptoms is needed to quantify these tools. Namely, Symptoms 10, 17, 24, 26, 27, and 28 are critical. Further, additional insight is given by comparison to Macro-Tool M12, Forward-Aged Margin Dollar Content in Order Backlog.

The output of the use of these tools is the pinpoint identification of sources and extents of operating pre-tax streams; where the firm is doing OK and where it is hurting. Note that Tool M11 uses the term "representative" rather than "salesman." The more inclusive term is used so as not to exclude agents and other types of authorized representatives which the patient firm may employ.

Micro-Tools m1, m2, m3, m6, m7, m8, m9, m10, m15, and m16 should also be used in combination with these three tools to insure optimal perspective of data behavior and to bolster validity of the eventual selection of curative treatment.

**M12.  Forward-Aged Margin Dollar Content in Order Backlog**

This is a unique tool. It is the *only* tool that applies accounting data, directly and at once, to the construction of the run-rate forecast. These are the only data that directly bring reality to future performance projections. The more reality that can be incorporated in the run-rate forecast, the more realistic and legitimate will be the objective forecast resulting from "subtraction" of the run-rate forecast from the target forecast.

This powerful tool injects cold-eyed realism. How is that power exercised? It is well known that sales can only be made *after* orders have been entered and accepted. It is equally well known that there is always a cycle time interval between order acceptance and shipment. Thus, the order backlog, if analyzed properly, will reveal minimum shipment potential *and* the margin dollars that can be realized from those shipments on a month-to-month basis into the future. The most frequently encountered and most often used period is the "month."

The normal or traditional approach to preparing a run-rate margin forecast is to take the "average" of actual margin achieved in the recent past and project it into the future. Use of this tool, however, allows you to project *actual* margin dollars that will be realized as the already booked order backlog is shipped. It is almost invariably the case that the future actual margin will be *less than* the projection of the recent past "average."

Review of eroding gross margin data (Symptom 10) will verify why this is so. A firm in a genuine turnaround will display a pattern of erosion of gross margin. And, it should not be surprising to learn that the pattern of erosion will extend into the near term future. In other words, things were getting worse and will get worse yet as time goes by if we fail to do something about it!

On the other hand, if—glory be—this tool reveals a flat or rising margin potential month after month, the firm may have already bottomed out and may even be on an upswing.

How is this tool prepared? First, analyze each line item for each order in the backlog to determine (1) the "normal" cycle time interval to shipment for that item, and (2) its margin dollar content. Second, post each line-item margin dollar content to the columnar future week in which the shipment is likely to occur. The shipment week is identified by adding the "normal" cycle time to the date that the order was accepted and entered. Third, total the future week columns in which the line-item margin had been earlier posted. Finally, accumulate the columnar totals into months; calendar or four-week, five-week fiscal periods.

A few additional comments will be helpful. Of course, use approximation to ease preparation and computation. Once this tool has been documented, insist on continuation of its preparation on a regular, usually weekly, basis. Not only will it provide continuing evaluation of the run-rate margin forecast, it will first reflect the results (if execution was professional) of many of the remedial actions that were taken.

This tool also provides a sure-fire method of quantifying many operational management tasks embodied in the objective forecast. How so? Well, if you view order backlog as a type of inventory, then orders represent input; sales or shipments represent output; and the backlog itself represents the account balance. Thus, *all* sales forecasts must presuppose order input. If sales exceed order input, the backlog balance will fall. If monthly sales exceed monthly order input for any lengthy period, the backlog balance will vanish. In other words, the objective sales forecast, to be credible, *must* be supported by a credible order input forecast. While shipment forecasts are always a joint effort by marketing and production personnel, the marketing personnel should stand alone with order input forecasts.

All that has just been said about sales forecasts applies with equal vigor to margin forecasts, of course! If the objective forecast calls for margin improvement over the run-rate forecast, and it always will, the needed improvement must first be visible in the new order input as it enters backlog. Again, for the margin forecast to withstand interrogation, the planned margin improvement actions and the timing of those actions must likewise withstand interrogation.

## MICRO-TOOLS

### m1. Product Line Gross Margin Percent Profitability

Specifically, the analysis we seek is a hard-copy listing in descending sequence of gross (or standard) margin percent of each product line. Note that for this micro-tool and many other micro-tools, we ignore the traditional *accounting-type* sequence fields. That is, for optimal use, we disregard product line number or other accounting systems classification nomenclature. The gross margin (or standard margin) percent field is exclusively used for sequence control.

Sorting the product line unit records in descending sequence is the key to effective diagnosis. By sorting the data in that sequence, you will quickly be able to draw a line below which the margin percent becomes unacceptable. Also, with time at a premium, you can rest assured that you will *not* overlook a more favorable margin percent farther on in the listing.

Having thus separated the firm's product lines into acceptable and unacceptable, all you need do is concentrate your attention on those below the acceptable margin percent line. In one simple data listing, you will know which product lines are hurting the firm and which are helping. Only those "below the line" will be later included in the selection and application of remedial actions.

### m2. Product, Model, Catalog Number Gross Margin Percent Profitability

There is a refinement of Micro-Tool m1. Normally, model and catalog numbers are accumulated into product line subtotals. This micro-tool deals with and presents the more detailed product data prior to accumulation into product line.

Again, this listing is sorted in descending sequence by gross margin (standard margin) percent. In effect, this micro-tool breaks up product lines into the winners and losers *within* the product line. You are thus enabled to identify particularly onerous individual products, which in turn very likely will enable you to take more easily managed remedial action. The value of smaller, incremental remedial actions is elaborated in Section V.

This micro-tool will flush out the individual winners and losers that otherwise would escape your knowledge if only product line subtotals were relied upon. There most probably will be cases where a product line may barely pass acceptable margin muster only because a few individual products are doing spectacularly well while hosts of others are doing poorly.

### m3. Cumulative Margin $ by Product, Model, Catalog Number

This total consists of a relisting of the same data file as that used to generate Micro-Tool m2 above. However, here we focus on the year-to-date, prior year, or other meaningful time period and the number of gross (standard) margin *dollars* realized during that period.

Two features of this analysis are noteworthy. First, sort the detailed data in descending sequence of number of margin dollars. Second, cumulate, line by line, the number of margin dollars and print the running cumulative total in a separate column. A particularly useful refinement can be included: If the total margin dollar amount is known prior to the preparation of the listing, divide it into each successive, new cumulative amount and print the resulting percentage adjacent to the respective dollar subtotal.

Upon completion, you can visually and instantaneously

observe the extent to which Pareto's law is operative. The basic rule of thumb, of course, is that 80 percent of the margin dollars will be generated by 20 percent of the number of products. This micro-tool, then, provides a meaningful partial answer to the first of the two questions that all professional managers continually ask, "Where does the money come from?"

Again, initially draw a line across the listing at, say, the point where 80 percent of the margin dollars are accounted for. Then, compare the products identified below that line with the "below the line" products identified with Micro-Tool m2 above. The resultant merged list of losers provides the menu for the product pruning remedial action that will assuredly ensue.

### m4. Direct Labor Compensation $ as Percent of Sales

Where the format of Micro-Tools m1 through m3 was a listing of period summary product performance, the format of Micro-Tools m4 and m5 is a listing of period-by-period data behavior. It is a time-series exercise. Probably the most useful period is the quarter or approximate three-month intervals if the firm uses a thirteen-week fiscal quarter, for instance.

What you should be looking for is the behavior of the ratio over time. Is the ratio increasing, stable, or decreasing? If it is not stable, how great is the favorable—or more likely, unfavorable—deviation from historical levels? What does the trend line reveal? How fast is it rising; what are the characteristics of the most recent changes; what caused any favorable flex points in the curve; and so on.

With this tool and with Tool m5 below, "compensation" includes both direct and indirect payments. That is, it includes both pay (salary, wages, commissions, fees, and so on) and fringes (vacation, insurance, pension, and so on).

Ideally, this curve should resemble a straight line with a downward slope. Such a curve says that productivity gains have consistently outpaced increases in compensation. In turnaround situations, however, you will *never* see such a curve. You will see the reverse. The curve will slope upward and probably at an increasing rate. Symptom 11 will show you by how much.

Study of the curve will allow you to make reliable projections of the curve's behavior. The curve's behavior can be easily translated back into dollars of cost. These estimates, in turn, provide useful input for cash flow and income statement forecasts.

Don't overlook the possibility of impact on the curve caused by product mix changes. While not probable, a shift in volume from acceptably profitable to proportionately more unprofitable can affect the curve. Use of Micro-Tools m1 through m3, Symptoms 10 and 25, and Macro-Tool M12 will provide reliable gauges and measures of any product mix shift effect.

The curve also may be rising only because sales are falling. Symptoms 9 and 27 will reveal the extent of that influence. If that proves to be the case, it can be safely inferred that (1) direct labor population has not been quickly enough reduced (Micro-Tool m30), (2) inventories are rising, and (3) cash has been dissipated by unwarranted inventory-type purchases. It may (and often does) also mean that operating profits have been overstated by unjustified overabsorption of burden expenses and that cash was again dissipated on injudicious increases in variable burden expense (Symptoms 13, 14, and 15).

The more that you practice building bridges of inferences, the more proficient you will become. The payoff of that expertise, of course, is that you will ever faster be able to pinpoint the problems and causes of financial distress; thereby enabling you quickly to initiate adequate, relevant, and effective curative treatment.

**m5. Indirect Labor Compensation $ as Percent of Sales**

The personnel included in this tool are all of those not included in Tool m4, above. In other words, here we seek to evaluate the compensation impact of all personnel who are not related directly to production of the firm's goods or services.

The comments about relevant inferences and format made with respect to Tool m4 apply equally here. One additional point that must be made is that special focus or attention should be given to any foreknown major compensation element. That is, if, say, pension costs or insurance costs are particularly high (or low), a more detailed analysis should be made in order to (1) isolate that element to ascertain later whether comparative shopping will result in a lower cost, and (2) remove the disproportionate, aberrational effect on the behavior of the ratio.

One final note: If the proportion of people employed in "below the gross margin line" functions (e.g., sales/marketing, finance/administration, engineering, and so on) is relatively large with respect to total population, this analytical tool should be prepared twice. First, include only operations-related indirect personnel. Second, include only the "below the line" personnel.

### m6. Customer Gross Margin Percent Profitability

Earlier, with Tools m1 through m3, we began to answer the key question, "Where does the money come from?" With Tools m6 through m9, we finish answering that question.

We begin by subtracting product costs from customer invoices to arrive at gross (standard) margin percent for *each* product invoice line item. Over a meaningful volume period, say, prior year or year-to-date, all of the sales to each customer are costed out, totaled and margin percent calculated. The listing is then made in descending sequence of margin percent. This format places the most profitable customer at the top of the list and the least profitable (more likely most unprofitable) customer at the bottom of the list.

A line can then be drawn at the minimally acceptable margin percent. Thus, those customers "below the acceptable margin percent line" constitute the agenda for either

(1) remedial action or (2) customer pruning. *Note:* Usually, the "$n$th" percent of market share really isn't all that profitable!

This tool is useful, too, to refute arguments for retention of unprofitable products on the too often spurious basis that retention of those products is necessary in order to retain this or that customer.

### m7. Customer Gross Margin $ Profitability

While percentage insights are always valuable, the diagnosis must always get to DOLLARS. Owners and creditors never heatedly and anxiously inquire about "percent per share." With this tool, we focus on the gross margin dollars.

Re-sorting the data used in Tool m6 into descending sequence of dollar amount, we instantly can see not only who of our customers generate profitable margin, we can learn, as well, the extent of loss dollar volume. We shall have identified those customers who help us and those who hurt us.

### m8. Cumulative Gross Margin $ by Customer

The final refinement in the array of customer-related gross margin tools is closely akin to the format used with Tool m3 earlier. Dividing the total gross margin realized in the time period under examination into the individual customer's total gross margin results in the percent proportion that the customer generates of the total gross margin that the firm received from all customers.

Sorting, then, in descending sequence of "percent of the total" field, and subtotaling each successive line, we obtain a listing which, by simple straightforward visual observation, reveals the extent to which Pareto's law is operative. Do 20 percent of the firm's customers generate 80 percent of the total margin received? Who are they? And who are the 80 percent of our customers who are causing our losses?

## MARKET SEGMENT OR DISTRIBUTION CHANNEL

It is very often the case that the firm does not deal with "repeat" customers, especially if it deals with either capital goods or noncapital durables. Or, while customers may "repeat," the cycle time or interval between orders is sufficiently long to distort time-period comparisons of results. If your turnaround patient does indeed deal with such customers, what should be done? Customer characteristics such as these seem to destroy or seriously impair the value of Tools m6 through m10. But, they really don't pose an impediment to effective diagnosis and prescription.

Instead of focusing on individual customers (or in addition to focusing on individual customers) we focus on market segments or channels of distribution. Market segments may be geographic: regional, national, international, and so on. They may be user-oriented: consumer, industrial, commercial, and so on. Channels of distribution used by the firm may include any or all of the following, and probably even some not listed: direct salesmen, agents, reps, stocking distributors, jobbers, wholesalers, retailers, and so on.

In other words, if trying to obtain insight by customer doesn't make sense—i.e., isn't useful—don't do it. Remember, what we're trying to get a handle on is where the dollars are coming from. If we can't define it directly by customer, then let's use market segment and/or channel of distribution.

The following three micro-tools employ the same format as that used with Micro-Tool m8.

### m9. Cumulative Gross Margin $ by Region

The primary sort is descending sequence of gross margin dollars, subtotaled by region. The region that generated the largest number of gross margin dollars will head the list.

As with Micro-Tool m8, showing the percent of total gross margin to the firm that each region generates will display the extent of operation of Pareto's law once again.

### m10. Cumulative Gross Margin Dollars by Sales/Marketing Channel

Using the same format as in Micro-Tool m9, we subtotal gross margin dollars by distribution channel. The resultant listing displays the relative contribution by each channel to the firm's total gross margin.

**m11. Cumulative Gross Margin $ by Representative**

With the subtotal print control for each representative, the resultant listing displays the relative contribution by each representative to the firm's total gross margin.

## DYNAMIC MARGIN

In many firms, you will find that it is "normal" to spend considerable sums on performance of the sales/marketing function. Reference to Symptom 17 and Micro-Tools m21 and m22 will quickly tell you if you are dealing with such a firm. If you are, then limiting your examination to the gross margin level will overstate the sources of operating pre-tax. If your patient firm does *not* spend such considerable sums—then *disregard* Micro-Tools m12, m13, and m14! They won't help you and all you will do is waste money and, worst of all, waste time!

What we seek to do is to obtain a measure of product profitability that takes into account both the cost of production and the cost of selling/marketing that product. So, what we will do is, first, subtract product cost from net sales to obtain gross margin in the conventional way. Second, we subtract sales/marketing expenses from gross (standard) margin to arrive at what we will call, arbitrarily, *dynamic margin*.

Why not? That seems like a good name and it certainly appeals to the sales/marketing types. After all, what could possibly be wrong or misleading about anything called "dynamic"? In any event, that's the number that we're after in the following three Micro-Tools.

One final comment. While Micro-Tools m12, m13, and m14, are labeled "Product Line," don't be restricted by that label. Remember that our basic premise was that significant sales/marketing dollars were being spent, so it *will* pay to arm ourselves with dynamic margin tools. But, *if the sales/marketing expenses cannot rationally be allocated to product line, try then to allocate by customer. If that doesn't work either, try region, channel, or representative.*

Note the repeated use of the word "allocated." It will prove to be a rare case, indeed, if you find that the firm's accounting system has already been collecting data in these classifications. Chances are that if they had been doing that earlier, your appearance on the scene as the company doctor would have been unnecessary. So, using approximation and sampling, do your best to "tag" the products, customers, channels, and so on with their respective fair share of sales/marketing expense. You will get a much more penetrating and illuminating insight if you do.

**m12.  Product Line Dynamic Margin Percent Profitability**

**m13.  Product Line Dynamic Margin $ Profitability**

**m14.  Cumulative Dynamic Margin $ by Product Line**

These three micro-tools are jointly presented because of their strong respective format resemblance to Micro-Tools m6, m7, and m8. There is no need to repeat much of that relevant and appropriate material. Please refer back to each of the earlier ones if these micro-tools are applicable to the firm under your examination.

## PERCENT OF SALES RATIOS

One of the most illuminating and useful analytical ratios, particularly when dealing with costs and expenses, is the proportion of the firm's total sales represented by each major cost or expense. With a few caveats in mind, these ratios can tell you a great deal about the answer to the second perpetual question, "Where does the money go?" A "percent of sales" ratio speaks to the size of that cost/expense slice relative to the firm's total revenue pie.

What are some of the caveats? Let's talk about them before we talk about how to use these ratios. First of all and back to basics, the ratio consists of a numerator which is the cost/expense under consideration and a denominator which is the booked sales revenue for the same period as that used in the numerator. Errors can creep into both numbers. Sometimes the errors can be sufficiently large to distort the resultant ratio value and, thus, may lead to incorrect inferences, conclusions, and actions.

The most common source of numerator error is alteration, modification, or change in the content of accounts and subaccounts. These changes usually reveal themselves in the form of a "step function" if the ratio is graphed over a time period that includes the implementation of the change. From time to time, it is normal for a firm to reclassify its accounts and subaccounts. It is *not* important that changes in account content have been made. What *is* important is that the changes are accommodated when you compute the ratio for a number of time periods. *Consistency is the key.* Even if the account content is somewhat erroneous, keeping the error constant is equally as important as eliminating the error. And error elimination is far more difficult to achieve than is consistency.

That caveat raises another important point. The true value of the "percent of sales" ratios is not what the number may be in any point in time. Rather, their analytical value lies in the behavior of the curve they display when graphed or plotted over successive time periods. The time periods, of course, should always be of equal interval. Whether it be week, month, or quarter, once you've decided on an interval—stay with it. If it proves to be the case that the chosen interval fails to display meaningful curve behavior, then change the interval consistently for all data plots.

Use the same time interval when projecting the ratio curve into the future. It is important to use the same interval for all of the different "percent of sales" ratios so that curve data comparability will not be impaired. While the change, over time, of the behavior of any one ratio is of course important, its behavior relative to other associated ratios will provide unique, additional insights that single ratio analysis alone cannot deliver.

The major caveat, however, deals with the denominator, the firm's reported total sales. First of all, only use net sales because gross sales are inflated, often, by nonrevenue elements as discussed earlier—see Symptom 9.

Second, if prices rose or fell dramatically during the period being analyzed, be sure to adjust the denominator values properly. It is more important to remove price increase effects than price decrease effects because the resultant ratios will be more conservatively stated thereby. Don't ignore price decreases—but don't sweat pinpoint precision.

When you construct a time series of ratio values for more than twelve months, it is possible that you may have included (or partially included) the effect of a product mix shift. It's OK to include it, provided that you have otherwise accounted for it in your analyses. Keep checking Symptoms 9, 10, 26, and 27 to make sure that you really understand denominator behavior.

All right, we've talked about the basic caveats and the most effective format, namely the time series. The longer the time series the better, because you can then track more easily where the firm has been. Are there any general rules or principles that we should be aware of as we examine the time-series plot? There sure are! Very seldom will you find that the curves rise early and fall in the more recent past. Remember that we're dealing with cost/expense ratios. If they rise, it means that the cost/expense that we're examining is taking a larger share of the sales dollar. If it is falling, it means that less of each sales dollar is so expended. And, if the firm we're dealing with really is in a turnaround, it will be a rare instance indeed where we will find a cost/expense taking less of each sales dollar.

So, by and large, the best performance that we can expect to see is a bunch of "horizontal" straight lines.

Most likely, what we *will* see is a large group of cost/expense curves rising—and rising faster per time period as we approach the present.

Don't try to read precision into the curve. It's not important whether the "horizontal" line is exactly horizontal. It's not important that there are minor peaks and valleys. You're really interested in the *overall pattern* of the behavior of the ratio as revealed by the curve. It's like an EKG. One or another minor aberration can safely be dismissed from consideration. View the curve as a whole and concentrate on its entirety. Keep in mind the conventional quality control chart; you know, the one that plots actual deviation points from the nominal performance or QC specification. The nominal line is bracketed by two acceptable or tolerable error limits, one plus and the other minus. So long as the actual data fall within these two parameters, quality is deemed to be "under control." And, the trend line of the actual data postings is far more managerially important than one or another spasmodic data point that falls outside of the control limits.

Pay special attention to "flex points." These are points along the curve where it changes direction. If it had been rising and then began to fall, find out what the hell happened. Ten to one you'll find an accounting reclassification of some kind. But, maybe not! You just may have found a second- or third-level manager who was really trying to do something about the sorry state of the firm's affairs. *Flex points always mean something happened.*

The discussion below dealing with Micro-Tools m15 through m29 is based on the premise that the denominator—the firm's net sales—has been verified, adjusted, and is relatively error-free. For each of the Micro-Tools, I will focus on behavior of the numerator and the inferences that can be drawn from ratio behavior. For reasons mentioned earlier, there is really no need to consider inferences related to a stable or a decreasing ratio value. Just count your blessings! Only rising values really need to be discussed.

The presentation also presumes a time series of at least twelve months so that seasonal effects, if any, are visible.

Finally, once you have constructed the curve plots, insist that they continue to be prepared. They will be extremely useful to pinpoint favorable change flex points as your remedial action takes effect. They will be very useful, too, in the preparation of the run-rate forecast portion of the turnaround plan. They can also be used, in many cases, to plot the objective forecast requirements.

### m15. Product Material Cost as Percent of Sales

In general, with relatively constant unit volume and mix, the cost of materials has risen and is rising faster than the unit selling price. Margins should show corresponding erosion (see Symptom 10) unless there are favorable offsets in product labor and product burden costs (see Micro-Tools m16 through m20). Check to see whether there have been changes in the accounting valuation of material leaving inventory for inclusion in cost of goods sold calculations. If so, there should have been a similar and offsetting change on the input side of inventory (see Symptom 23).

If the increase is significant and especially if it looks like it's accelerating, anatomize the material cost to ascertain which 20 percent of the elements constitute 80 percent of the cost increase. Is material substitution feasible? Trace the major material cost increases to the vendor. Ascertain whether and to what extent comparative shopping was performed. If none, personally negotiate with vendors and potential vendors for the top five or so largest material cost elements.

Check to see whether an ECO (engineering change order) increased the unit amount of material. If so, can the lesser amount be reinstated or was the increase caused by a legal conformance requirement of some sort?

### m16. Product Direct Labor Cost as Percent of Sales

If the firm uses a standard cost system, so-called, the amount of labor cost should always be the same value for each like unit. Therefore, an increasing ratio value can signal only a falling sales volume. Sales are falling (see Symptoms 9 and 10) either because prices are being cut lower and lower (see Symptom 10) and/or physical volume is falling (see Symptom 27), and/or a product mix shift is occurring.

If the firm does not use a standard cost system, it nevertheless may be the case that sales *are* falling for the reasons cited above. More labor dollars per unit may also reflect increases in direct labor pay (see m4, m33, and m36) with no appreciable offsetting change in productivity or efficiency. It may mean less efficient labor if unit sales levels are holding up (see Symptom 27). Finally, it may mean that a product mix shift is occurring.

In most cases, regardless of the cost system in place, it will reflect a combination of falling prices, lesser units, less efficient labor (because population was not reduced fast enough), rising inventories, and overstated operating pre-tax because of the questionable favorable burden absorption accompanying the inevitable and predictable inventory build.

### m17. Burden People-Related Variable Expense as Percent of Sales

An increasing ratio simply means that the indirect population had not been maintained or sufficiently reduced to properly correspond to the prevailing operational levels. If sales have indeed fallen sufficiently far, it may be that a total restructuring of the indirect personnel organization is necessary to eliminate now unaffordable support services in an orderly way. Micro-Tool m36 should show only zero, or perhaps only a trivial amount.

### m18. Burden People-Related Fixed Expense as Percent of Sales

If there has been no expansion of fixed-expense type activity causing corresponding higher population levels, the increasing ratio value is probably more reflective of decreasing sales than increasing population-related expenses (see m34 and m36).

If sales have fallen or probably will soon fall sufficiently far, a reevaluation of the extent of supportable, affordable plant facilities must be made—and made quickly (see m31 and m32).

### m19. Burden Plant-Related Variable Expense as Percent of Sales

An increasing ratio value can be caused by falling sales. Pursue earlier comments in that regard to verify authenticity of that inference. It can also, and probably does, reflect increases in the expenses associated with plant operation at levels higher than those required or justified by prevailing sales levels. Use Macro-Tool M5 if the increases are significant enough to be worth your while. Brace yourself; you will be seeing many more references to M5.

### m20. Burden Plant-Related Fixed Expense as Percent of Sales

Existence and/or continuation of plant operations in its present configuration becomes more suspect as this ratio increases. Profound questions are, and should be, raised as the ratio reaches what you feel may be alarm levels.

Combinative use of M5, m31, and m32 will help answer them.

### m21. Sales/Marketing People-Related Expense as Percent of Sales

The sales/marketing population has not been properly reduced to match the pattern of falling sales. That is what you will find most often to be the case. Check to see if there is a commission plan in effect which continues to pay higher commissions irrespective of sales level behavior. Don't laugh—I've seen more than one. It may be that commissions are paid on booked orders; if so, check M12.

### m22. Sales/Marketing Other Expense as Percent of Sales

Symptom 17 offers special help here. It may be that some of the expenses—promotion programs, advertising, and so on—really shouldn't be cut. I never did, nor ever will, subscribe to the "management by thrashabout" notion that all advertising and sales promotion programs should be automatically cut back or eliminated when dark financial clouds first appear on the horizon.

In any event, further examination cannot be disregarded. Put M5 into action so that you will clearly see where most of the dollars are going.

### m23. Finance/Administration People-Related Expense as Percent of Sales

Using the M5 approach, ascertain which are the major contributors to the expense increase. The general observation *must* be that the population has not been quickly enough reduced. Probe to see whether all the work being performed is truly essential. Or, is the firm incurring excessive expense so that it can measure its losses with great precision? I once knew of a firm where excessive expense was incurred and "justified" on the basis that "The books are being closed *much* faster. Before, the figures weren't available until the seventeenth or eighteenth. Now we get them on the ninth!" So what? All they revealed was losses—and the CEO was a gutless wonder who failed even to try to do anything about it.

### m24. Finance/Administration Other Expense as Percent of Sales

As stated earlier in Symptom 18, special attention should be given to interest payments. Review the debt instruments to see whether they provide for floating or fixed rates. Are rates going up? Are they likely to rise further? How far will they go in the next twelve months? Is the debt principal increasing?

Don't neglect other major expense elements. Use Macro-Tool M5 to identify the, say, top five or ten subaccounts; i.e., those five or ten that contribute or generate 80 percent of the expenses.

**m25. Engineering In-House People-Related Expense as Percent of Sales**

**m27. Engineering In-House Product-Related Expense as Percent of Sales**

These two micro-tools are presented together because of joint applicability of the following discussion.

Macro-Tool M5 will rank the major causes of expense for you. Symptom 19 names eight principal people-related expense components. Equally important to Micro-Tools m25 through m28 is the expense authorization documentation search. Why does the firm employ the population that exists? What are they working on? What are their projects? Who authorized and approved those projects? What are the goals and objectives of the projects?

Continue the pattern of interrogation through all of the major expense components for both people-related and product-related activities. Why was this or that equipment purchased rather than leased? What is the level of equipment utilization? How much "frosting" is included on the equipment? Review Symptoms 19 and 21.

**m26. Engineering Contract People-Related Expense as Percent of Sales**

**m28. Engineering Contract Product-Related Expense as Percent of Sales**

Again, these micro-tools are presented together because of the joint applicability of the discussion.

In addition to the earlier comments in m25 and m27 above, contract expenses (both people- and product-related) require special interrogative efforts. Specifically, thoroughly explore the contract file as it now exists. Again, remember that you're dealing with a firm in financial trouble—a turnaround. Expect to find excessive "informality," incomplete records, missing data and files—a general disarray. You will only rarely be disappointed, because that condition is one of the causes of the firm's trouble. If records had been kept current and in place, and the organization had operated with more discipline, there would probably be no need for your help.

Nonetheless, you bear the obligation of trying to reconstruct as best you can. Restudy Symptoms 20 and 22. Adapt the M5 approach to focus on the specific contracts and projects that are the major sources of the increasing expense.

### m29. Warranty Expense as Percent of Sales

If warranty expense is increasing as a percent of sales, something is most seriously amiss, *unless* there is a bona fide, demonstrable increase in technological content of the product or there has been a specific type of product mix shift. Product mix behavior is the first thing to check on. Compare what you learn about it to Symptom 27.

Trace the authorization/approval chain. Who makes the decision, *prior to* incurrence, that warranty expense should be incurred? Are decisions being made properly?

Did changes in personnel or procedures occur prior to or coincident with the noticeable increase in expense? What is the firm's published (or contractual) warranty obligation?

Use M5 to tell you where the major amounts of expense are being spent. Which products? Which customers? Does M2 and/or M7 shed further light on where (and why) the money is going? What is the approval procedure regarding incurring travel expense? Who authorizes the travel? Who audits the resultant expenses? Travel is very often a significant portion of booked warranty expense and again, very often, it is somehow overlooked. Abuses will occur in inverse proportion to the amount of inspection and scrutiny that is performed.

There is a possibility that this ratio is increasing only because sales are falling and expenses continue to be incurred proportional to earlier, higher-level sales. There is an expense "overhang." This possibility can be relatively easily checked out by pattern comparison between Symptoms 9 and 27, Macro-Tool M12, and use of the M5 technique on warranty expense subaccounts ranked by either product and/or customer. By and large, it's not very likely that you will find "overhang" to exist at all, and if it does, its effect will be minimal and should not be prolonged. But, since it's easy to do—check it out.

Trace the source or cause of major warranty expense attributed to a specific product or customer. Is the expense incurrence a one-time event or is it prevalent and ongoing? Are warranty expense-causing products under current remedial study by the engineers? Are they included in the engineering project workload? Are corrective actions known? Are they in progress? If not, why not?

Finally, is the firm meeting (but just meeting) its legal obligations with respect to warranty? Or, has professional objectivity somehow been lost as personal relationships between warranty service personnel and customer personnel have become excessively cordial? Are warranty service personnel identifying too much with the customer? There have even been cases, you know, where service personnel have become "silent partners" with the firm by selling pilfered parts and subassemblies directly to the customer at "bargain prices."

If warranty expense incurrence is traceable to customer-originated change orders, have those change orders been properly administered? Did the customer and the firm each do what was called for in the contract provisions? Was the firm properly compensated and/or reimbursed for change order work performed?

### m30. Sales Dollars per Employee

This is another rough gauge of productivity. The ratio amount at any one point in time has no particular analytical value. Rather, the performance of this ratio over time can reveal useful insights. Use of this Micro-Tool combinatively with m4, m5, m17, m18, m21, m23, m25, m33, and m34 will yield the greatest analytical value.

There are two avenues of pursuit. First, a study of the behavior of the curve over time can generate useful questions. If the curve is falling (the most common pattern found in turnaround situations), it is most often the case that the number of employees has not been reduced in a timely manner. Sales dollars in a turnaround situation almost always are falling. So, unless employee population is correspondingly reduced, the ratio value must fall.

The higher the technological content in the product, the higher the ratio of sales dollars per employee should be. The converse is equally true. A good rule of thumb to start with is the range of $30,000–$40,000 per employee. This range should be appropriate for a firm whose products have about average technological content. Compare the ratio value of the firm under examination to this rule of thumb and obtain plausible answers for significant deviations from it. Also, once you obtain the "proper" range for your firm patient, use the ratio in reverse to tell you about how many employees *should* be on the payroll at varying sales levels.

### m31. Sales Dollars per Plant Square Foot

Many of the comments made about Micro-Tool m30 are equally applicable here. This is yet another productivity measure that is more valuable and useful when used in combination with others (m32, for instance) than when viewed in isolation.

The starting point rule of thumb is a range of $40–$50. As technological content of the product increases so does the ratio value. As more production, manufacturing, processing are performed in the plant, the ratio value tends to decrease somewhat. Not to worry, though. Remember, *volume is nothing—margin is everything!* As more and more product manufacture is performed in-plant, the opportunity for margin improvement increases. A turnaround situation indicates that that opportunity has not been exploited. It's up to you to exploit it optimally in your Turnaround Plan. The ratio can reach or exceed $100, and often does, as the use of automation increases. A tip-off is a very high m30 ratio value.

### m32. Capacity Utilization Percent

This micro-tool, obviously, has almost exclusive applicability to manufacturing firms. You will learn in a later section that one of the most powerful remedial actions that can be taken is to increase capacity utilization. Not only does improved utilization (1) lower the firm's break-even point, (2) lower unit costs and (3) in some cases even lower fixed costs; it achieves one more very important objective. The key to a successful turnaround is enthusiastic execution of a professional Turnaround Plan. The key to enthusiastic execution is a well motivated operating organization—*people!*

Improved capacity utilization allows you to retain selected operating personnel. You will be able to afford to keep the people that you want to keep in both the "variable" and "fixed" job functions. The ability to retain an experienced cadre strongly enhances the probability of a successful turnaround. Note that I did *not* say to keep *all* of the incumbents. In extremely rare cases you may find it profitable to do so, but generally you will find a shortage of skill and talent among the incumbents rather than an abundance. After all, the firm *is* in a turnaround and *somebody* had to put it there. It is highly unlikely that all of the operating personnel are free of culpability. On the other hand, it is also highly unlikely that all operating personnel are culpable. So, a crucially important element of your management of the turnaround will be your selection of personnel for retention.

Please restudy the capacity utilization discussion in Section I. It will avoid repetition of that material here.

The most important point with respect to quantification of this micro-tool is the "capacity" definition that you choose. Unless there are overriding circumstances—for example, the firm patient is a process-oriented firm and round-the-clock operation is virtually economically mandatory—the most useful definition is:

> The unit output produced by one day shift, five days per week in all departments and work stations adjusted by the run-rate level of labor efficiency.

Note that *unit* output is used rather than dollars, thereby enhancing consistency and ease of comparability. Only one shift, the day shift, works only five days per week. The run-rate of labor efficiency is a necessary adjustment. If labor efficiency is unknown or questionable, use 80 percent as a start point. Test the reasonableness of that rate by dividing direct labor population data into Symptom 27 data for the respective time periods. Adjust the rate as the results of the comparison warrant.

However the utilization is derived, a very useful figure is obtained by calculation of additional unit (or sales dollar) capacity *potential* which is the difference between measured utilization and 100 percent. Much more of this discussion will follow in Section V.

**m33. Compensation $ per Direct Labor Employee**

**m34. Compensation $ per Indirect Labor Employee**

These are basic reference data. Construct a time series for each and study the curve behavior. The direct labor curve should approximate the average hourly rate for forty-hour weeks for a firm in a turnaround. How does the average hourly rate compare to the industry or to other nearby comparable jobs?

If the labor force is unionized, the curve should show step-function jumps corresponding to the pay increase provisions in the contract.

Micro-Tool m34 provides you with a reference point for comparison with other micro-tools dealing with employee compensation. If you think that a great deal of attention is being paid to employee compensation, you're right! It is not unusual to discover that total employee compensation is in the range of 30–40 percent of sales, and sometimes even higher. It is truly difficult to become too knowledgeable about this huge slice of the revenue pie.

**m35. Overtime Premium $ per Direct Labor Employee**

**m36. Overtime Premium $ per Indirect Labor Employee**

Given that we're dealing with a turnaround, both of these averages should approximate zero. Overtime premium dollars should be tolerated *only* when it is *clearly* demonstrable that (1) the work to be performed is necessary, (2) it must be performed at the time identified, and (3) avoidance of hiring additional full-time employees is amply cost justified.

Trace the authorization/approval chain. Who authorizes overtime? On what basis is it authorized? Is it authorized before or after the fact? How is the scheduled work to be performed, monitored, and audited? And so on.

## SECTION V

# REMEDIAL, RESTORATIVE ACTION

### Overview

This section warrants an overview of the decision criteria that *should* control your selection of actions to be taken. We will deal here with a truly critical step or phase in the turnaround management process. For the very first time in this *Handbook, you* decide to DO something to cure the firm patient. *Now* is the time when *you* must select *action* to be taken. Until this point, you have been, essentially, a data gatherer, a learner, an interrogator, and an inference chain builder, or at least you should have been all those things. Others have come to you with reports, answers, responses, chitchat, and even gossip.

*No more!* The time has now come for you to choose what must be done. Not only must you identify the prescription, you must specify the strength of the doses and how long the treatment must continue. Only Section VI of this *Handbook* is more important than this one. There you will see to it that the diverse treatments which you selected here are blended and combined into an effective therapy. Further, you must persuade the owners/creditors and the operating organization that your prognosis will be effective. You must even get the patient to take its medicine enthusiastically.

If you absorbed the earlier sections in this *Handbook,* you now possess and have displayed the degree of aggressive patience that is the hallmark of a true professional. You are well prepared to make judicious and prudent choices. You will indeed be able to throw out *only* the bathwater.

As you take the thirty-one actions described here, maintain running records of the individual and cumulative effects of those actions on the firm's cash and profit outlook. Use a twelve-month calendar and post the effect of *each* action taken on a month-of-occurrence basis. The value of this record can hardly be overstated. You will reap great benefits in Section VI as you will soon see.

If you fail to capture the effects of the actions as they are defined and quantified, you will lose track of the progress that you have made toward meeting or exceeding the target forecast.

The firm didn't get into trouble because of a single, lone big-dollar blow. Don't expect to find a single, lone big-dollar action that will cure the firm. Most likely, you will need scores of relatively small-dollar actions to save the firm. Consider yourself fortunate if you do in fact face that most likely scenario. You will see why when you get to Section VI. The future twelve-month calendar of expected results is and will be your most powerful single management tool!

And, finally, *review* the Action/Turnaround Stage Relevance Charts in Appendix 6.

## DECISION CRITERIA

### The Crucial Difference Between Costs and Expenses

A sound understanding of the difference between costs and expenses will significantly aid the action selection process. This discussion is *not* intended to be accounting theory treatise, nor does it seek to receive unconditional endorsement by the AICPA. It *is* intended to provide you with insights into prevalent real-world practices and relationships.

*Costs*

Costs are usually cash expenditures related to balance sheet items. They tend to be part and parcel of the basic ongoing business. An example will help. Direct labor, the manual effort devoted to "hands-on" production of the firm's goods, is a cost. The dollars spent on this activity are incorporated into the accounting value of the product, the accounting value of inventory. They are a principal element of the products we removed from inventory and shipped to a customer. As direct labor dollars are incurred, they are deposited in the inventory accounts on the balance sheet.

Another characteristic of costs is that they tend to remain about the same per unit of product irrespective of changes in operating levels. In other words, if your firm is in the business of making and selling widgets, the direct labor cost per widget will remain about the same over any short-term or even medium-term period. Further, the direct labor cost per widget will remain about the same irrespective of the number of widgets produced and sold during that time period.

Costs tend to be "sticky" in the sense that they are not easily reduced. The amount of material in a product will remain about the same unless there are design or other engineering changes that can safely reduce the material unit content. But the "gestation" period for design or other engineering changes tends to be lengthy rather than brief. Money (sometimes truly major sums) must be spent to make favorable changes in costs. Reducing labor cost by purchase of automation equipment can require large sums indeed—and lengthy implementation periods.

In brief, costs are usually associated with two of the Three P's: product and plant. Expenses are usually related to the third "P"—People.

While cost reduction can and usually does favorably affect cash flow, it is usually the case that cost reduction is pursued to enhance the quality of profitability of the firm. Let's take a moment to distinguish between the objectives of improving (1) profit, (2) profitability, and (3) cash flow.

## Profit, Profitability, and Cash Flow Improvement

*Profit* improvement action aims primarily at increasing the *quantity* of profit in the short and often medium term. Profit quantity improvement can usually best be achieved by reducing expenses. Profit improvement usually concurrently improves cash flow but the improvement rarely is long lasting. As the firm regains its financial health, the expenses are not only usually replaced, but very often they are replaced at an even higher level.

*Profitability* improvement action aims at improving the *quality* of the firm's profit, often in the medium term but usually in the longer term. Profitability improvement is usually best achieved by reducing costs. Profitability improvement very often does *not* improve cash flow in the short or even medium term because cash outlays are required, say, to acquire automation equipment (to reduce labor cost), close or relocate plants, complete engineering projects to achieve material substitution (to decrease material cost), and so on. On the other hand, when the cash flow improvement is finally captured, the effect tends to be long lasting.

## Expenses

Expenses are cash expenditures usually related to income statement elements other than the "bare-bones" cost of goods sold line. That is, income statement line items such as the variances in cost of goods sold—labor, material, and burden—really *should* always be considered and treated as expenses. Always be slower to capitalize burden variances than either labor or material variances.

Expenses tend to vary in amount per unit of product. In fact, they are almost always completely dissociated from unit levels. The money will be spent on, say, the advertising program regardless of current unit volume levels. After all, the goal of the advertising expense should be to increase unit volume in the future.

Expenses tend to be "slippery" in the sense that they can be turned on or off, increased or decreased, relatively easily. Engineering project expenses can be delayed or even canceled with the stroke of a pen. A person can be hired or laid off relatively quickly. Expenses tend to be under "subjective" control; they are only rarely truly integral to "being in the business."

Because of the nature of expenses and given either a cash crunch or cash shortfall turnaround situation, expense reduction action almost always gets priority attention. And, in those circumstances, debt service or interest expense coverage usually is at the top of the remedial action list.

Expenses are associated, to a very large degree, with the third "P"—people.

### Less IS More!

As you weigh and ponder selection of remedial, restorative action, don't for a moment forget that *other* people will be given the assignments of implementing and executing those actions. No matter how hard you try, you just simply won't be able to do it all yourself. And even if you foolishly tried, you'd probably botch it; there's just too much to do. The old bromide still has plenty of fizzle: management *is* the art of getting work done through the efforts of others. Turnaround management *is,* after all, management. So, identify and define actions in such a manner that they are easier for others to execute rather than more difficult.

The more discrete the action steps, the more quantitatively defined they are, the simpler the assigned task; the smaller the bite, the easier it is to swallow. Management tends to be better—that is, easier—if numerous small tasks are prescribed rather than a few sweeping general assignments that criss-cross organizational lines. The more easily a subordinate can "put his arms around" his task, the greater will be his understanding of what's expected of him. The greater that understanding, the more likely it will be that it can be performed successfully.

Consistent with the ancient wisdom that it's easier to catch a whale with a 1000 small hooks than it is with only one big hook, a program consisting of many small tasks will make it easier to achieve enduring turnaround success than one sweeping "management-by-thrashabout" bleat to "cut *all* expenses by $n$ percent."

Be mindful, too, that execution is always imperfect. Therefore, if the goal is to, say, reduce expenses by $100 because the firm is facing a cash crunch, it will always be better if a dozen easily understood $10 tasks are undertaken than if only one vague, complicated $100 task is generally assigned.

### When You're In Command—COMMAND!

Webster tells us that to command is "to direct authoritatively." And a leader, he says, is, "a horse placed in advance of the other horses of a team." You know, the more that I think about it, the more I really like his definition of a leader. It will do you no harm at all to think of yourself thus if you have the good fortune to have been entrusted with a turnaround management responsibility. Pay particular attention to the last phrase, "... of a *team*." If we blend the two definitions, an effective turnaround manager (or *any* effective manager for that matter) is one who authoritatively directs his management teammates.

Specifically, though, in a turnaround situation, what early, positive, authoritative, and visible action *should* you take? First and foremost, *do* as little as possible, at least until you've measured the symptoms, evaluated them with analytical tools, and built strong inference chains. But, *learn* as much as you can about the Three P's in the firm in as short a time period as you possibly can.

The most effective method you can use to place yourself quickly in the mainstream of the business is to personally approve all of the requests for cost and expense expenditures. On Day One of your assignment, direct that until further notice *all* cost and expense authorizations will require your *personal* approval. Yes, I said *all.* Purchase order requisitions (both for inventory and noninventory items), overtime requests, hires (whether of direct or indirect labor), fires (again whether of direct or indirect labor), travel advances, planned travel (insist on approval of itineraries at least one week prior to scheduled departure), warranty, wage and salary increases, and so on. Also, direct that *all* of the firm's checks will require your signature. Given these directives on Day One, you will have served notice to the organization that you are, indeed, the "horse in advance of the other horses." Second, you will have given yourself the opportunity to review and interrogate every transaction that generates cost or expense before that cost/expense is incurred.

*Caveat*

Go extremely slow in the exercise of rejection or disapproval of the requests that appear for your review. Follow the football adage: Always give 'em the short ones; don't ever let 'em have the bomb.

DO NOT go slow, however, with interrogation. Place the burden on the requester to explain why a particular request is necessary and should be approved. You'll become very knowledgeable very quickly. If the amount of the request is relatively large, and you're facing a cash crunch or cash shortfall, don't reject it. Instead, negotiate that it be either (1) delayed in total or (2) delayed in the major expense or cost items.

If an engineer, for instance, requests a major amount and tells you that the project is required by sales/marketing, call in the head of sales/marketing *immediately* to ask for an explanation of the pressing need. In short, don't let them treat you like a ping-pong ball!

### Communicate!

The more that the operating organization knows about what is going on, the less time that will be wasted on fruitless counterproductive speculation. Uncertainty is worse than misinformation because uncertainty always breeds only anxiety, polarization, and stress. Uncertainty always generates a more negative frame of mind than is really warranted. A positive, "can do" attitude goes a very long way toward making the turnaround effort a success. The first step you should take to build that attitude is to convince your teammates that you are all in this thing together and that it's really up to all of you to turn the firm around. The easiest way to begin the process is to broadcast your own "open door" policy. Be available. It's far better to be an early "arriver" than a late "stayer." Most people by far are more productive in the early hours.

Hold group meetings regularly with all employees, union leaders, supervisory personnel, and management personnel, as well as one-on-one encounters in the office and on the plant floor. Start the first general meeting with the positive announcement that although the firm does have problems, you and the owners are dedicated and committed to resolving them as quickly and fairly as possible. Tell people what to expect: that changes will be made *after* management is sure they really know what they're doing; that everyone faces a learning process; that there will be data gathering, reports, analyses; that problems will be defined very carefully; that *their* input is important.

Assure them that you will keep them informed as the process progresses. Keep that promise, for sure. They will thrive on feedback. Solicit their help, cooperation, ideas, and recommendations. Urge them to come forward with what they view as problems that the firm faces. Level with them. Don't blue-sky; don't soft-soap!

People don't learn anything until they realize they have a problem. And fear not that your people will become defeatist as they learn of the dimensions of the serious problem faced by the firm. They are far more resilient than you might imagine. They'll throw in the towel only if you allow them to feel they're somehow out of it; that they're not really part of the action.

As the symptoms become clearer, as the run-rate forecast begins to assume shape, as the target forecast is finalized, be quick to make sure that the management group, especially, really understands what the problems are; that they understand just how big are the gaps between the two forecasts. If you fail to get their attention you won't stand a snowball's chance of pulling off a successful turnaround.

Don't fail to communicate to the market! If there are customers, distributors, wholesalers, agents, and others who are truly important to the firm's success, meet with them one-on-one during *Week One* of your tenure. Don't wait or delay. They know that the firm is in trouble and establishing rapport with the new "top guy" will give them a real boost. Chances are, they will be quick to tell you of the firm's problems as they see them. They seldom need encouragement to tell you what they think or how they feel. Unfortunately, their tale of woe will seldom vary from the three "perpetual problems": "Prices are too high! Quality is lousy! Delivery is too long!" (You've heard them before, have you? Well, brace yourself. You're about to hear them one more time.)

### Confidence

If *you* don't exude confidence, nobody in the organization will have any at all. It's as simple as that. And the best part of it all is that you don't ever have to fake it! A well-prepared, well-executed turnaround plan *never* fails. Take heart!

Under the direction and inspiration of a "pro," the organization will soon begin to show all the zeal there is in a firm and an organization that is "born again." There really *is* a latent "phoenix effect" which, if kindled and nurtured, will become the driving force as the firm and the organization take wing once again.

Finally, let me share a piece of priceless advice that I received about twenty years ago as I was about to assume my very first assignment as president–general manager. Even if I do say so myself, it was a tough first assignment. It was a multiplant, multiproduct operation. My mission was threefold: to consolidate the plants, to consolidate the organizations, and to measurably improve *both* quantity and quality of profit in twelve to eighteen months. I'm happy to report that my mission was fulfilled.

I was told, "Dick, there are only two ways to do anything. You can do things graciously, or you can do them ungraciously. And, you know what, it doesn't cost one red cent more to do them graciously!" So, my friend, as you select the actions to be taken, be mindful that virtually every one that *you* choose will affect the lives of employees and their families—a lot of people. Try your utmost to do it graciously.

## REMEDIAL, RESTORATIVE ACTIONS

Presented below are thirty-one possible remedial actions that you can take. You may think there are more—and there probably really are. Most of those not included below are simply not feasible—for example, "Increase equity by enough to bail the firm out." The remainder really don't help the firm to survive with its identity and ownership intact—such as, "Sell the Firm." The assumption in this *Handbook* is that the firm, while it faces serious problems, has not been allowed to deteriorate to the point where its infirmities are fatal. If the firm *can* be turned around, professional use of this *Handbook will insure* its survival.

Let's briefly review the four stages of a turnaround. In terms of immediacy and urgency, they range from cash crunch to cash shortfall to quantity of profit to quality of profit. The basic differentiation between the stages is the time period in which the continued survival of the firm faces dire jeopardy. The time periods associated with each stage below indicate the amount of time left before financial disaster:

| | |
|---|---|
| Stage 1. Cash Crunch: | NOW! |
| Stage 2. Cash Shortfall: | 3–9 months |
| Stage 3. Quantity of Profit: | 6–12 months |
| Stage 4. Quality of Profit | 9–18 months |

Corporate health is not really all that different from human health in the sense that if symptoms are ignored, early corrective treatment is precluded and the patient's condition becomes increasingly worse. If management fails regularly to examine the prospects for corporate health nine to eighteen months into the future (i.e., to test for quality of profit problems in its future income stream) it will soon show symptoms of quantity of profit problems. If these, too, are ignored, a cash shortfall stage will surely eventuate and, unless action is promptly taken, survival will soon be in jeopardy as the firm reaches the potentially terminal cash crunch.

Consistent with the sequence of presentations of the symptoms, the remedial, restorative actions are presented in descending sequence of immediacy of financial disaster. In other words, the actions correspond, generally but not exclusively, to the turnaround stages as follows:

| Turnaround Stage | Remedial, Restorative Actions |
|---|---|
| 1. Cash crunch | 1–6 especially, and 7–19 generally |
| 2. Cash shortfall | 1–6 somewhat, but 7–15 especially |
| 3. Quantity of profit | 7–15 generally, but 16–19 and 25–27 especially |

4. Quality of profit     7–19 and 25–27 generally, but
                         20–24 and 28–31 especially

Finally, before we get into detailed discussion of the "how" of each remedial action, let's make sure that we really understand the "why" of taking action. Of course, we want to keep the firm alive and its ownership intact. More specifically, though, how far should we go with action? How much is enough? For example, we may decide to reduce employee population; but all the way to zero? Clearly not. Somewhere between the existing population level and zero is the "right" number. How do you select that number? Where do you stop? How do you tell where the bathwater leaves off and the baby begins?

Refer back to Figure 1. Note the dotted line interval on the left side which begins with Step 1 and ends just after you begin working on Step 5, Quantify Remedial Actions. It is during this period that you should finish, at least, the drafts of the run-rate forecast and the target forecast. When the run-rate forecast is "subtracted" from the target forecast, the "differences" comprise the objective forecast. The objective forecast, then, fills the "gap" and identifies the required extent of remedial action for each line item in the forecasted financials: cash flow, income statement, and balance sheet.

Because the symptoms and the remedial actions are (how fortuitous!) also expressed in terms of financial statement line items, so that they can correspond directly to the objective forecast. Thus, for example, if the objective forecast shows that sales/marketing people-related expense must be reduced by the equivalent of one full-time person, don't plan on laying off two or more, *unless,* after rigorous examination, the additional personnel were redundant anyway under the circumstances.

To sum up, the reason why you choose one particular remedial action or another is that it is an appropriate and necessary element to build the bridge between the run-rate forecast and the target forecast. And, the length of the total span of that bridge is (should be) the effective limitation on the extent to which that remedial action is applied.

Refer frequently to the appendixes. In particular, become very familiar with Appendix 5, "Action/Symptom/Analytical Tool Interreference Table," and Appendix 6, "Action/Turnaround Stage Relevance Charts." Appendix 5 provides complete, detailed cross-references. Discussion of each Action below will only touch on the most important/useful symptoms and tools. Careful study of Appendix 6 will sharpen your understanding of the relevance of each Action to each of the four turnaround stages. For each action, you can easily observe the Stage in which that action will have the greatest effect.

OK, let's get on with it.

## "IMMEDIATE" CASH FLOW IMPROVEMENT

Remedial Actions 1 through 6 seek to get cash into the corporate coffers QUICKLY! The cash crunch has hit. Lenders have stopped lending. Suppliers have stopped supplying. Payroll is due the day after tomorrow. The patient is hemorrhaging, for chris' sake! If you want the firm to have chance of survival, don't waste a second inquiring about how it all happened. You'll have time for that later, *if* the firm survives the crisis. What you want to do can be stated very simply—GET CASH! Symptoms 1 through 7 and Macro-Tool M12 pretty well spell out the degree of urgency that is required.

## 1. "Fire-Sale" Inventory

Sometimes considerable cash can be obtained by severely marking down inventory and dumping it on the market. The better the reputation of the product and the firm in the past, the more likely this approach is to succeed. But at a price. This action may so taint the firm and its products that an entirely new "image" may later have to be established. But better to have to build a new image for the firm than a coffin.

Generally, likelihood of success—that is, garnering significant cash—is inversely related to the technological content of the product. The greater the general use of the product, the easier it is to move in a "Fire Sale." "Nuts and bolts" are much easier to peddle than, say, special purpose electromechanical subassemblies.

You will also find it the case that raw material and piece parts are easier to dump than either work in process (usually subassemblies) or finished goods. And, it's easier to dump finished goods than work in process. So, examine carefully the inventory profile of the firm patient to make valid assessments of "Fire Sale" potential.

Who can we sell the stuff to? Competitors are often the best prospects for the sale of raw material. Distributors are often the best prospects for piece parts because they can resell them later at truly attractive margins. This is particularly true if the products involved are either capital or noncapital durables. With those products, there is usually a favorable cost/benefit trade-off for the user to repair and maintain rather than dispose and repurchase.

The less that the ultimate user knows about your "fire sale" the better. There is always a strong possibility of a backlash effect where both the firm and its products are shunned by "fire sale" prospects because they view it rather as a "going out of business" sale. The least likely adverse effect on sales will result from the dumping of raw material.

As you embark on this action, you will encounter two pricing arguments. The first holds that, since you can always drop price further a little later, don't initiate the sale at too low a price. The counterargument says that (1) after your "hold back" pattern of pricing has been discerned, prospective buyers will also intentionally hold back purchases in anticipation of yet lower prices; (2) it may take too long to go through successively lower prices and you will fail to generate enough cash early enough.

The second argument says, "Drop your pants right now! Price at or even below book value. Move the stuff. Get the cash and move along to the next thing." Except in rare circumstances, I find the second argument far more persuasive. It tends to be effective rather than efficient. It may not get the last dollar of sales that otherwise might be obtained, but it does afford a far better chance of getting "95 percent" of that total *quickly*. And, if there ever was a time value of money, it sure as hell is high when you're in a cash crunch.

Symptom 23 may present you with either an opportunity or yet another problem.

## 2. Factor Accounts Receivable

In effect, this action is a "fire sale" of the firm's receivables. You "sell" them at a discount. Usually a deep discount is extracted. This is, by and large, not a very good source of cash. If the firm is in a cash crunch, it is highly likely that the "good" receivables have already been collateralized. Lenders usually are willing to supply cash for 80–90 percent of face value of solid, reliable customers.

The remainder of the receivables are not as desirable. The anticipated payment rate can plummet particularly if these marginal credit risks sense that the firm may be going out of business.

The total dollar amount of receivables will probably not be very high to begin with. Sales have probably fallen and more probably have fallen severely in the recent past. But, with survival of the firm at stake, don't fail to overlook or pursue any feasible remedial actions.

### 3. Renegotiate Union Contracts

This action is more often associated with quantity or quality of profit turnaround stages. It's presented here because far too many quantity or quality of profit stages are not recognized promptly enough and acted upon. Too many turnarounds are allowed to erode to cash crunch and, thus, the cash crunch stage is the most frequently encountered by the company doctor.

Whether or not they have been formally informed earlier, rest assured that the union leadership *is* aware that the firm has serious problems. Bring them in promptly, nonetheless. Lay out the problems and prospects in as full detail as is possible. Since the firm will probably soon be in breach of some of the contract provisions anyway, (Symptoms 3, 5, and 6 principally), you have nothing to lose by calling for renegotiation. And, you might have much to gain! The union leadership *is* vitally interested in maintaining jobs. That's the only way they have to keep membership up. And, that's the only way they have to keep those union dues rolling in every month, don't you know.

But here is a situation where "big" problems are better than "little" problems. If the firm has a relatively small union population, the international is likely just to write it off. But, if you're a Lockheed, Chrysler, GM, or Ford, well now, that's a horse of an entirely different color. In short, your clout with the union is directly proportional to the number of union employees. Obvious, right? Right!

## 4. Renegotiate Credit Lines and Debt Service

Good Luck! If the firm is already in a cash crunch, it has also probably exhausted the patience of the formal lenders. After all, that's part of the definition of a cash crunch. But, it just may be the case that you were brought in by them to fix things up in the first place. Well, that just might be your trump card!

As you draft and finalize the lenders' portion of the target forecast, you may be able to persuade them that things *will* get better. The lenders only want their money. They do not want to "take over" an operating firm—particularly one with financial problems. That's not their business; their business is to make money by lending money. They want the firm not only to survive but to grow and to flourish.

Your goal is to strike a balance between the target forecast demands and stretching out payments as far as possible. The end result of these negotiations will be a payment schedule that lies somewhere between complete pay back tomorrow to complete pay back years in the future.

With regard to increasing the firm's credit lines, the initial hurdle that you will face is answering the question, "Why should we throw good money after bad?" A well thought out, documented Turnaround Plan will go a long, long way to answering that question. Therefore, don't vigorously pursue this action until you have at least a semifinal version of the turnaround plan. If you're asking for a larger credit line, you must (to be successful) be able to demonstrate how the increase in the credit line will be a key factor in restoration of corporate health.

### 5. Renegotiate Vendor Terms

Your personal eyeball-to-eyeball contact is mandatory. Here again, remember that vendors take no glee in turning down orders. They take no glee in turning off customers. They want to sell to your firm. But they want payment, too. Who knows, maybe they read this *Handbook* and *you're* at the top of *their* customer pruning list.

How to proceed? Start off by identifying the top half dozen or so vendors who are truly essential to the success of your Turnaround Plan. Then, as early as possible establish contact with their top people. (By the way, I know that you will not have finished your Turnaround Plan at that point, but you sure should be able to identify those vendors that you really need by examination of Macro-Tool M12, Gross Margin Content in the Forward-Aged Order Backlog report.) Introduce yourself; tell them frankly of your mission and assignment. Listen carefully to their view of past relations with your firm. Begin to develop, with them, their target forecast demands.

Your goal is not only to get vendors to forego their (usually) rightful demands, but to obtain their pledge of support and cooperation to make the turnaround plan successful. They really want you and your firm to succeed. But they cannot ignore their obligations to their owners, nor can they help if their role is unknown to them. Again, press for your vendors' future support only after you can present them with at least a semifinal version of your turnaround plan.

The more they feel that they have a role to play, a voice, an input, the more they will identify with you and your firm. COMMUNICATION—a businesslike, frank, candid, honest yet cordial, informal relationship—is as essential with the vendors as it is with owners, creditors, management personnel, and employees in general.

The success of this action, as with Actions 3 and 4, hinge crucially on your personal impression. Make no bones about it. Forget cold-eyed, objective, arm's length impeccable logic. By itself, it simply won't work. Of course, prepare and present programs that can withstand searching scrutiny, but don't forget that, at the outset, all you have to "sell" is yourself and a future promise.

### 6. Reduce Purchases

Finally, an action that you can initiate internally within the firm. If, on Day One, you took my earlier advice and issued a directive that all purchase order requisitions must be personally approved by you, you will have gone a long way to reducing purchases.

Your goal is to *avoid* spending even one truly unnecessary dollar. Remember, it's always better to initiate your management tenure with overcontrol rather than undercontrol. You can always ease up on procedural requirements (to the applause of the operating organization) but it's practically impossible to tighten the screws later and leave the organization intact. Also, if you follow the latter course, the owners/creditors just might get the idea that you weren't really all that sure of yourself after all.

The firm makes only two types of purchases. There are purchases of "inventory" items that go directly into the product. And, there are non-product related purchases. With regard to the "inventory" purchases, approve *only* enough to match the shippable booked order backlog. Forget about quantity discounts!

Don't "purchase" direct labor and indirect labor to make parts, subassemblies, or finished goods that are not absolutely needed for shippable booked order backlog. Ignore the income statement effect of underabsorbed burden expense. This Action pursues *cash,* not profit. Reducing burden expense, which also reduces the adverse underabsorption effect is coming up next.

Approval to spend money on non-inventory items should be very, very difficult to obtain. Be realistic; you will not be able to get those purchases down to zero. Don't try to wring out the last dollar—you'll waste too much time and effort on small impact items. Again, if you are able to shelve 90–95 percent of the proposed purchases, you will have done a whale of a job!

Finally, don't forget to exercise approval control not only before the money is *spent* but even before the *obligation* to spend the money is made. If the firm doesn't use purchase order requisitions or cover all expenditures with purchase orders, install both procedures right now! You won't need fancy forms—probably couldn't afford them anyway. Just get the word out fast, "Don't even think of ordering anything until you've got my OK."

## REDUCE PEOPLE-RELATED EXPENSE

Actions 7 through 12 deal exclusively with employment layoffs and terminations. This is the principal realm of action that has "immediately" favorable effects on both cash and profit. Many managers also find this to be the toughest realm of action because it means personal confrontations—looking someone in the eye and saying, in effect, "You no longer have a job here." These actions tend to be emotionally laden. If they are mismanaged, severe harm can befall the prospects for turnaround success because it is dependent upon the performance of the remaining operations organization. Aside from some general advice—level with the people, be honest, try to help relocate, avoid hasty or premature decisions, and be as gracious as you can—there are several specifics that warrant emphasis.

First, terminations involve severance payments. Some severance payments, e.g., for union personnel, are contractually defined. Thus, the favorable financial effects of terminations, with rare exceptions, are somewhat delayed. Therefore, where possible, stretch out the severance payments to conserve cash. Where possible, make the severance dependent upon re-employment and avoidance of action harmful to the firm. Perhaps, as part of Action 3, the union severance pay provisions can be favorably renegotiated.

For nonunion personnel who may have employment contracts with the firm, attempt to negotiate a stretchout of severance payments. Finally, check both union and employment contracts carefully to ascertain whether severance payments can be deferred if the termination can be handled as only a layoff. If so *and* there is likelihood that the personnel may be recalled, utilize those provisions, of course.

Try to add to the enhancement of the firm's survival by careful employee selection. Select for retention those individuals who will most likely contribute to the success of the turnaround, irrespective of that person's tenure. Tenure, moreover, never equates to experience. Do not retain anyone only because he's been there *so* long. Often one of the big reasons why the firm is in trouble is that personnel turnover has been woefully insufficient. No surprise; that's usually why you find so much "deadwood" in a sick firm.

Make sure that each employment termination is well documented. One of the fastest emerging areas of labor law is "wrongful" or "unjust" termination. If improperly handled or if improperly motivated, the firm and its officers and directors can be subject to suit by the wrongfully discharged employee. Federal laws prohibiting discriminatory discharges are mirrored in many state laws. Actions can be, and have successfully been, brought in civil suits bottomed both on contract and tort law theories. The firm may be exposed to damages for both the decision to discharge the employee and the manner in which it was conducted. Use experienced counsel to oversee the planning and the implementation of these actions. With all of the operating problems that you already face, you sure as hell don't need more inadvertently caused problems.

Terminations are upsetting to the organization. Everyone would like to see things just continue on as they have been. You will never fail to get a rise out of your listener when you say, "There will come a day when there will not be a single incumbent left on the payroll." Turnover, 100 percent turnover, is inevitable. Professional managers only control the extent and the timing of it for the best advantage of the firm. But personnel changes are upsetting nonetheless. While anxiety, turmoil, and upset cannot be completely avoided, there are a couple of ways that they can be mitigated.

First, get it all over with at one time if you can. It's far better to have only one "Black Friday" than to have them occur weekly. The sooner that those who are to be retained know that their jobs are secure, the better. The sooner that the termination action is completed, the sooner the organization will recover from the shock of it, and the sooner it will stop wasting time and energy in speculation, rumor, and gossip about "Who will get it next?"

Second, notify the individuals about whom decisions have been made as soon as possible. People naturally want to know where they stand. Don't keep them hanging. Not only is prompt action beneficial to the affected employees, it is also beneficial to the firm. It's always better to initiate cash and profit improvement sooner rather than later.

Don't limit terminations to the personnel identified for discharge in the objective forecast in order to reach the target forecast. If, after examination, there are personnel who can be discharged without placing the firm's recovery in jeopardy, of course proceed with those discharges also. If you fail to take that additional action you send fuzzy and conflicting signals to the organization. If you tell the organization, that all personnel who are not key to the success of the turnaround plan will be discharged, as you should have, then apply that criterion pervasively but consistently. Don't kid yourself. The organization knows pretty well who are the "good" people and who are deadwood or worse. If an individual has no foreseeable future role in the firm, it is really in his best interest, too, to move on as soon as possible.

Obviously, exceeding the objective forecast requirement provides insurance that the target forecast will be hit. An excess above the objective forecast generated by any of the remedial actions can give you the latitude to fall short of the objective forecast in some other area if it's judicious to do so. For example, you may find that it is more beneficial for the firm to expand a sales promotion program funded by the surplus achieved with Actions 7 through 12, or others.

Finally, keep in mind that Actions 7 through 12 deal with all people-related expense. Salaries, wages, and commissions are only a subset of those expenses. When quantifying and calendarizing the effects of these actions, be sure to include the favorable effects associated with reductions in fringes, perks, travel, education, supplies, and so on. It is not unusual to find that these nondirect compensation and expense elements can approximate and in some cases even exceed the total direct compensation. Similarly, be sure to include the adverse effects of severance payments, extended insurance coverage, and other cash or profit related severance arrangements.

With all of these introductory remarks in mind, let's take actions, shall we?

## 7. Reduce Variable Burden People-Related Expense

The results of quantification of Symptom 13 pretty much define the parameters of feasible expense reduction action. Recall that the personnel we're talking about, essentially, are "on the plant floor" but not directly involved in production of product. They "support" the direct labor, "hands-on product" efforts. They are material handlers, forklift truck operators, stock pickers, and so on.

The theory is that this population should rise and fall in rhythm with direct labor population. But operating management is notorious for failing to see to it that the indirect labor population does indeed drop in sync with direct labor population drops. When the direct labor population drops, indirect labor personnel do not voluntarily rush lemming-like for the exit. Management must take the initiative. Sometimes, one finds games being played by plant managers who are under pressure to reduce the indirect labor population. Population data are usually measured in terms of full-time employees assigned to one classification or the other—direct or indirect. Don't be surprised, upon deeper interrogation, to find part-time indirect personnel on the payroll. And, be sure to check into the direct labor diversion account. No, this account does not refer to the recreational activities of the direct labor personnel. It is, or certainly should be, used to record the dollars of expense incurred by personnel who are formally classified direct labor but who actually perform indirect labor type work. Thus, when the COO puts pressure on the plant manager to reduce indirect labor, don't be surprised to see indirect labor population fall—and direct labor diversion rise.

Effective expense reduction action, then, focuses on *dollars,* not population. Of course population data are indicators, but make sure that you've got your hands on the dollars being spent. Because of the large fringe benefit costs associated with retention of a full-time employee, there *may* be an expense trade-off advantage to reduction of indirect labor population and intentional incurrence of part-time (fringe-free) labor expense and/or direct labor diversion. Usually, you will save some 30¢–40¢ of every such expense dollar.

Review the indirect labor roster carefully. Verify that employees are properly classified. Then, on a department-by-department basis, verify the need for retention of each individual. Use the "zero-base" concept; that is, start out with a zero indirect labor population and authorize retention *one at a time* as each compelling case is made. Make sure that the direct labor personnel that they support are working *only* on shippable, booked order backlog.

Reduce the other people-related expenses of the population that you finally decide to keep by exercising "before the obligation" control. Travel expense, for example, can almost always be reduced by scrutiny and interrogation of the proposed itinerary if presented to you a week or two prior to requested departure.

Micro-Tools m5, m17, m34, and m36 will measurably assist in action formulation. Macro-Tool M12 will be particularly valuable.

## 8. Reduce Fixed Burden People-Related Expense

Symptom 14 describes the job functions of this population, which generally does not vary or fluctuate with direct labor population. However, if decreases in operating levels are severe enough or are likely to be prolonged, expense reduction opportunities abound.

Macro-Tool M12 provides the data base from which appropriate population levels can be derived; by comparison to the existing population levels, the potential reductions can be relatively easily determined. So long as operating levels are focused on and restricted to shippable booked order backlog, you can rest assured that the fixed indirect labor population can be maintained at the lowest feasible level.

The associated people-related expense control comments in Action 7 apply equally here. Micro-Tools m5, m18, m34, and m36 provide quantitative monitoring and control measures.

## 9. Reduce People-Related Sales/Marketing Expense

Draw on Symptom 17 and Micro-Tool m21 to provide the basis on which to begin action formulation. Macro-

Tools M9, M10, and M11, augmented by Micro-Tools m9, m10, and m11 will direct you to the most promising expense reduction targets.

As you prepare the list of personnel for termination, evaluate each individual first in terms of reassignment from unprofitable products, channels, or regions to profitable ones. In other words, try to convert this seemingly otherwise defensive action into an offensive one by removing sub-par performers and replacing them with individuals of greater competence and/or potential.

The control and reduction of associated people-related expenses other than direct compensation has been extensively dealt with earlier in this *Handbook* and requires no repetition here. (For examples, see Symptoms 6 and 13 through 20; Macro-Tool M5; and Micro-Tools m5, m16 through 21, m23, m25, and m26.)

### 10. Reduce In-House People-Related Engineering Expense

Symptom 19 defines the characteristics of the population and the expenses under review here. Macro-Tool M12 and Micro-Tools m1, m2, and especially m3 and m25 provide highly useful guides for effective action formulation.

The minimum permissible expense level can be derived from combinative analysis of the Forward-Aged Margin Dollars Content in Order Backlog (M12) and the product profitability analyses. First of all you can and should direct that the level of the retained population will be determined according to the following work-load criteria:

1. Operations will be supported by engineering only to the extent of the effort necessary to insure completion of the volume of shippable booked order backlog
2. No engineering people-related expense will be incurred on unprofitable products (they will soon be pruned anyway) *unless* there is a quick, sufficiently inexpensive "fix" *and* there is demonstrable promise of significant, relatively near-term (i.e., less than twelve months) unit sales volume
3. No engineering expense will be incurred on new products *unless* demonstrable, compelling cash and profit improvement exists within the next twelve months *and* the target forecast cash requirements will have otherwise been met or exceeded.

"Fixing" unprofitable products may yield additional benefits beyond the sales-profit-cash benefits. Namely, check to see the extent to which inventory already on hand could be incorporated into the "fixed" product, if it were "fixed." The larger the amount of such inventory, the less "new" cash will be required for production and the greater the resultant cash realization from otherwise nonliquid assets.

For longer range considerations, after the firm has demonstrated its survival, establish project authorization procedures to plan and control *all* engineering activities and expenses.

## 11. Reduce People-Related Contract Engineering Expense

Symptom 20 provides the basic data with which to begin. Micro-Tool m26 provides additional insight. The only practical way to reduce these expenses is to cancel or renegotiate the contracts that obligate the firm. The basic criterion is whether the expense to complete is greater or less than the expense to cancel or postpone. The contract language itself will largely govern that decision.

Nonetheless, view these expenses, to the extent possible and permissible, in the same manner as that suggested earlier in Action 10.

## 12. Reduce Finance/Administration People-Related Expense

Symptom 18 gives you your starting point and Macro-Tool M1 along with Micro-Tool m23 provide quantification measures.

Generally, this is the population that directly contributes least to improved cash flow and profitability. But, they are also the only personnel who can provide reliable numbers. The criterion then becomes whether the expense to provide the numbers is greater or less than the value of the numbers provided. When the accounting cost exceeds the value of cost accounting, reduce the accounting cost. There is no sense at all in incurring accounting expense when the only tangible result is a very precise measurement of the firm's losses. And, since no amount of accounting can ever really reveal the actual cost of a firm's product anyway, use of Macro-Tool M2 and Micro-Tools m1, m2, and m3 will suffice. Consistent use of M5 will keep you focused on the major expense line items.

## REDUCE PRODUCT-RELATED EXPENSE

The following series of three remedial actions focuses on reducing product-related expenses, *not* costs—we'll get to those a little later. Generally speaking, this expense area offers few significant expense reduction opportunities. It is very often the case that expense reduction potential for any firm corresponds to the following pattern:

People-related:      80–90%
Product-related:     5–10%
Plant-related:       5–10%

Thus, even though product- and plant-related expenses together may constitute only some 10–20 percent of the total expense reduction opportunity, they are not a trivial proportion and should be aggressively pursued.

Product-related expenses sometimes find their way onto the balance sheet when firms capitalize compensation, supplies, models, test instruments, and the like. The usual routes are (1) burden compensation expense involving product quality control and depreciation related to equipment and so on used therefore, and (2) engineering compensation expense involving product "fixes," product modification and/or "new" product development, and depreciation related to equipment, models, prototypes, and so on used therefor. Analyzing the relevant symptoms will quickly uncover the relative significance of these items so that you can correspondingly prioritize your time.

Product-related expenses tend to cluster about the second and third aspects of product as defined earlier in Section I. They are, respectively, quality and availability. I have already touched on quality-related expenses above. Availability or service expenses include warehousing, transportation, warranty, delivery, support, training, installation, and so on. They are, unfortunately, a blend of people-related expense and non-capital goods and/or services. Some examples of the latter are sales promotion programs, manuals, tools, training seminars, product replacements, and so on.

The firm's functional personnel usually associated with these expenses include sales/marketing, engineering, and both variable indirect and fixed indirect operations personnel. Because these expenses are so fragmented and yet so interwoven, early and consistent use of Macro-Tool M5, Subaccount Analysis, will yield significant conservation of management time and effort.

### 13. Reduce Sales/Marketing Product-Related Expense

Symptoms 26, 27, and 28 will be most helpful in conjunction with Symptom 17. Macro-Tools M5. and M12. will provide the priority of expense reduction opportunities and the outlook for expense behavior as well.

The remedial actions rest, in most cases, on trade-off decisions. Some examples will help. Will cancellation of a sales promotion program benefit the firm more than capturing the additional sales expected from that program? Will the introduction and training seminar for prospective customers result in timely additional sales? And so on.

The decision criteria are not always easy to finalize. As a rule, the decisions tend to become more difficult in turnaround Stages 3 and 4 than in cash crunch or cash shortfall stages. Generally, the less cash that you have to work with, the fewer the viable options that you have. But *not always!* A particular sales promotion program, seminar, and so on may be just what the firm really needs to generate immediate cash. Expenses, professionally managed, are dealt with one at a time. To do otherwise is to succumb to management by thrashabout.

Within this category, it would be unusual to find that people-related expense represented a major portion of the total.

### 14. Reduce Product-Related In-House Engineering Expense

Symptom 21 is probably the most relevant. Micro-Tool m27 will tell you the proportion of this expense to the firm's total sales. That may or may not be meaningful depending upon the turnaround stage that you're dealing with and what Macro-Tool M12 reveals.

Again, you'll find a blend of people-related expense

and expenditures for supplies, tools, and so on. M5 will sort out the priority of attack for you. In the absence of project reporting procedures, M2 will prove most useful.

Some of the decision criteria are: (1) Is the firm legally obligated to customers to incur the expense? (2) Will the expense really generate incrementally rewarding benefits to the firm? (3) Can we afford a "total" failure to achieve the objectives of the engineering efforts? And so on.

### 15. Reduce Contract Engineering Product-Related Expense

Essentially, the comments made earlier in Action 11 apply equally here. The trade-off questions include (1) Is the expense of contract cancellation less than the expense of contract completion? (2) Will the "improved" product sales from contract completion generate more margin than the expense to complete the contract? And so on.

Basically, the provisions of the contract between your firm and their firm will limit the opportunity for expense reduction. Therefore, early in-depth familiarity with the contract will enable you to select a viable, yet rewarding, course of action.

## REDUCE PLANT-RELATED EXPENSE

This series of four actions aims at reduction of the expenses associated with operating the plant and facilities.

The premise is that the existing plant and facilities will be retained; that is, we do not here consider disposition of assets. That will come a little later.

You will find that people-related expenses are frequently interwoven with these expenses. But, to the extent that Remedial Actions 7, 8, 10, and 11 were implemented, the content of people-related expense in these areas will be correspondingly reflected. Generally, however, we will deal more with non-people-related expenses.

As a rule, the benefits of these four actions are not quickly realized. Implementation of some of them require negotiations with vendors and others.

### 16. Reduce Plant-Related Variable Burden Expense

Symptom 15 provides the starting point to measure the extent and pattern of expenses for supplies, maintenance, utilities used in the production process, expendable tools, and so on. These are expenses that *should* vary with operating levels. Therefore, Macro-Tools M2, M5, and M12 will provide useful perspective and insight. Micro-Tool m19 will be particularly useful, but m31, m32, m34, and m36 will also be of assistance.

Insisting upon your personal authorization control of purchases of these items will go a long way to reducing the expense. Tightening physical control over these items will enhance legitimacy of use—have you ever noticed the increased "use" of utility gloves every spring when home chores need to be done?

### 17. Reduce Plant-Related Fixed Burden Expense

With the premise that existing plant and facilities are retained, opportunities for significant expense reduction are few and far between. Nevertheless, they should be pursued not only to gain whatever benefits *are* available in the short term, but because the value of reductions made grows through time as the firm struggles through survival to growth once again.

Symptom 16 is the principal source of information about the extent and pattern of these expenses. Symptoms 2, 3, 16, 25, and 27 are also helpful, however. We're dealing, generally with expenses such as taxes, insurance, and the like. Perhaps tax rate reductions or "holidays" can be negotiated. The likelihood of success in such negotiations, by the way, increases as you deal more with local authorities. Perhaps relatively minor expenditures, such as smoke alarms, can favorably affect insurance rates.

### 18. Reduce Plant-Related In-House Engineering Expense

Typically, these expenses range from attempts to improve labor productivity to routine equipment maintenance. The trade-offs include questions such as: (1) If the firm is legally obligated to incur the expense, how long can it be postponed? (2) Will the anticipated gain from the effort sufficiently and quickly enough exceed the anticipated expense? (3) With modest expense, can the firm forego major expense; is there an affordable "band-aid" solution that will last until we're out of the woods? And so on.

Symptoms 2, 3, 15, 16, 25, and 27 all help to gain useful insight. Macro-Tools 2, 4, 5, and 12, and Micro-Tools m19, m20, m25, m31, m32, m34, and m36 provide needed perspective. Do *not* devote a great deal of time and effort to this action *unless* Macro-Tool M5 reveals *really* significant targets of opportunity.

### 19. Reduce Plant-Related Contract Engineering Expense

Similar to Action 15, the opportunity for expense reduction is largely governed by the contract provisions. However, whether it would be worthwhile to cancel or renegotiate the contract can be ascertained by the use of the same symptoms and macro-tools cited above in Action 18. Likewise, all of the Micro-Tools cited there are applicable here with but one exception: use m26 instead of m25.

## IF IT HURTS, DON'T DO IT!

Clearly, one of the modern day gurus of turnaround management is Henny Youngman. Speaking in parables, as all true gurus must, he spins the tale of the man who went to see his doctor. The doctor asked, "What's wrong?" The man, lifting his arm, said, "It hurts when I do this." The doctor thought a moment and admonished, "Then don't do that!"

How many firms have you seen who pay no attention to the lesson in that parable? They just keep on selling unprofitable products to unprofitable customers through unprofitable sales/marketing channels. The aim of the following five remedial actions is, simply, to "Stop doing that!"

In almost all cases where these remedial actions are implemented, sales volume will drop as the pruning process develops. Therefore, consideration must be given to the likely consequences from reduced operating levels or capacity utilization, unused inventory, and others.

Another common thread of these five actions is first to attempt to make them profitable before you prune them. In the real world, however, you will find only rare instances when that initial attempt will be successful or even be worth trying.

Usually you will find that only Action 21, Eliminate Unprofitable Customers, offers opportunity for significant savings in time to help cure a Stage 1 cash crunch turnaround. Generally, it will be the case that these pruning actions will generate increasing benefit in Stages 2, 3, and 4.

## 20. Eliminate Unprofitable Products

This action is also known as product pruning. The candidates for pruning are identified principally by combination of Symptoms 26 and 27, Macro-Tools M1 and M12, and Micro-Tools m1, m2, and m3.

The trade-offs include: (1) How much inventory would

we be stuck with if we dropped this product? (2) How easily could we dispose of that inventory by implementation of Action 1? (3) Do product-related expenses (sales/marketing, engineering, etc.) sufficiently exceed the potential inventory exposure? (4) Is there a probable risk of losing profitable customers (see Action 21 below) by failure to supply the needed array of product? And many others.

> NOTE: *Never try to implement this action without also being ready to implement Action 21, Eliminate Unprofitable Customers. Unless you are so prepared, you will be unable rationally to defend against the predictable sales/marketing argument for product retention on the basis that, "We'll lose this or that important customer if we fail to offer a 'full' product line."*

### 21. Eliminate Unprofitable Customers

This is a tough one. The resistance from sales/marketing management is often intense, usually prolonged, and sometimes rational. But, so long as a credible job has been done, principally with Symptom 28, Macro-Tool M12, and Micro-Tools m6, m7, and m8, you have an excellent chance of making true believers of them.

Do *not* overlook the possibility of converting the pruning candidates to profitability. The chances for success increase as sales/marketing expense per customer increases. Examine whether that customer is unprofitable at the gross margin line or at the dynamic margin line. If you can convert a customer from unprofitable to profitable by reduction of sales/marketing expense attributable to that customer—jump at it! Cut the expense. But, if the customer is unprofitable at the gross margin line, he's only buying your "loss leaders"; better to write him off.

How do you eliminate customers who are unprofitable at the gross margin line? First of all remember that what we would like to do is to retain the customer, but on a profitable basis. Now then, to the extent that Action 20 has been implemented, it just may be the case that the altered product mix will result in profit at the gross margin line. Failing that, see Action 25, Raise Prices! The unprofitable customers will usually eliminate themselves by ordering from another firm, who by the way is probably in a turnaround Stage 4, headed for a Stage 1. But that's their problem.

## 22. Eliminate Unprofitable Channels

What we examine here are the various ways that the firm's products or services are routed to customers. Some of the issues are: (1) Are there legal restraints that impair or restrict elimination? There usually are. (2) If there are, can they be renegotiated so that the suspect channel is once again profitable? Often, not always, they can. (3)

What will be the likely reaction by customers accustomed to being served by the eliminated channel? Generally the answer to this question is that since the customer has found it profitable to buy your firm's products or services in the past, he will continue to. But he will let you know, in no uncertain terms, that he will cease further purchases should "service" of his account suffer or deteriorate. In short, the market is not usually too shook-up.

The consequences of a channel elimination however, are usually far-reaching within the firm. Sales/marketing expenses, such as promotion material and advertising, can be eliminated. However, a key consideration with respect to expense reduction must be the assurance that the firm's customers will be at least equally as well served after elimination of the channel as before.

Raising the price of the firm's products or services to that channel such that it becomes profitable may very well implement this action. If distributors, for example, no longer find it profitable to carry your line, they will drop it.

Symptoms 10, 17, 14, 26, and 28 provide the tip-offs of channel profitability problems. Macro-Tools M2, M4, M8, and M12, and Micro-Tools m1, m2, m3, m10, and m22 provide corroboration and deeper insight.

### 23. Eliminate Unprofitable Regions

Regions or districts and other geographic areas tend to become unprofitable for either of two basic reasons. First, the sales/marketing expense in that region may have risen sufficiently to destroy the dynamic margin. Or product mix changes may have occurred that destroyed the gross margin generated in that region. Sometimes it's a blend of both, but not often. Usually, you will find that product mix is the culprit.

If the problem hinges on abnormal growth of sales/marketing expense, Actions 9 and 13 should suffice. If it's product mix, Actions 20 and 21 should handle it. But you may find the case where post-sale expenses—warranty expense—has punished profitability because of the distances involved. In other words, the product price is not sufficiently high to accommodate transportation and travel expenses required. It is expensive to make a service call in Bangkok if you're located in Cleveland.

Look for the same symptoms as those for Action 22. Also the same Macro-Tools apply, but use M10 instead of M9. And, use all of the same Micro-Tools, too, but substitute m9 for m10.

### 24. Eliminate Unprofitable Reps

Recall from earlier discussion of Macro-Tool M11 that included in the label "reps" are direct salesmen, agents, account reps, special consultants, and the like. In short, we're talking about those people who contact or "handle" the ultimate customers directly on behalf of the firm.

This action almost comes down to a performance evaluation of an individual. But, usually more than one individual is involved; and, occasionally this action escalates to "channel" elimination considerations as in Action 22.

If the rep had been profitable and then turned unprofitable, Symptoms 10, 17, 24, 26, 27, and 28, and Analytical Tools M2, M4, M11, M12, m1, m2, m7, m11, m22, and m29 will jointly and combinatively provide the wherewithal to determine severity, timing, and other relevant patterns associated with that change.

There are four possibilities that may explain the adverse change. First, unit volume may have fallen so low that it failed to cover sales/marketing expense (Symptom 27). Second, a product mix shift occurred resulting in an insufficiently high gross margin (Symptom 10). Third, sales/marketing expense increased sufficient to wipe out dynamic margin (Symptom 17). And, fourth, a combination of the three occurred. It's relatively easy to quantify all four with objective, impersonal data.

## GET SALES UP!

Sustained long-term growth is of course dependent upon sustained increasing sales. There is a plethora of books that purport to tell you how to conceive, initiate, and sustain a strong sales improvement offense. Here, we talk only about defense—how to increase sales, temporarily, with the aim of buying time so that the corporate patient will survive long enough to assure a "future"—long enough to turn the firm around successfully.

As Action/Turn-Around Stage Relevance Charts 25

and 26 (see Appendix 6) illustrate, the value of Actions 25 and 26 falls consistently after Stage 1. The basic aim of all three, however, is to give revenue a "shot in the arm"—to ease the immediacy of the demand for cash.

### 25. Raise Prices!

*Yes!* Raise prices! Across the board!

As with all actions, prudence is premised. Raise prices in such a manner that the firm avoids Robinson–Patman Act price discrimination complications, of course.

This action can be quickly implemented—and just as quickly reversed. Mobility is but one of the favorable characteristics of this action. Notify the channels, reps, and "key" customers prior to enactment. You know what to say, "Because of [complete the rationale in one hundred words or less], we find it necessary to raise prices by $n$ percent (pick a percentage that substantially contributes to meeting immediate cash needs) on such-and-such a date (select a date no more than thirty days in the future)." While you want the price increase to contribute substantially to meeting immediate cash needs, do *not* try to satisfy *all* the cash needs by this one action alone. Don't raise price so high that you further exacerbate the problem. Symptom 10 and Macro-Tool 12 will keep you on track—if you but heed them.

Another benefit of this action is the probability of a rush of orders to get the product at bargain prices. The counterargument to taking this action is that all you're really doing is stealing future—and presumably more profitable—business. But, so long as you're facing a Stage 1 cash crunch, who cares? If you don't cure Stage 1, there won't be a future. Further, if your firm survives to Stage 2 or beyond, you can always reduce price, prune unprofitable products, and/or substitute more profitable ones. A "hoped-for" rush of orders helps significantly to reduce otherwise nonliquid inventory and, to the extent that operational levels are raised, coverage of "fixed" burden expenses is enhanced.

Finally, this action goes a long way to support and complement Actions 20 through 24—the "pruning" actions. If unprofitable customers choose not to buy at the now profitable prices, they will have eliminated themselves for you. That consequence is similarly arrived at with channels, regions, and reps. In this latter consequence, however, rarely is it the case that affirmative management action will be unnecessary.

Even after Stage 1 is passed (Whew!), *continue* to raise prices. *Never price as a mark-up of cost!* If your costs are too high, you automatically price yourself out of the market. If your costs are below those of competition, you will fail to maximize margin. *Always* price at what the market will bear. Keep pressing price until you have intersected the price elasticity curve. Don't bother trying to draw the curve first, before you begin to take this action. It's not worth the time and money. Rather, let the real world tell you when you have crossed that line. Now, now. Calm down. Everything won't go to hell in a handbasket.

Raise price periodically in relatively small increments, say 4–6 percent. Don't raise price regularly every fixed time period, e.g., every six months. Customers will soon discern the pattern and adjust purchases accordingly.

When do you stop notching up and up? When the real world tells you to! When the forward-aged margin dollar content in order backlog (M12) reveals that *total* dollars have flattened out or dropped somewhat. Disregard market share considerations. The plain and simple truth is that, so long as total margin dollars are increasing steadily into the foreseeable future, you're doing OK. You might be able to do better by broadening the customer base (i.e., increasing share) by dropping price, *or* by product modification, *or* with acquisition, *or* whatever. The luxury of being burdened with selection from among healthy growth options can come only after the total margin dollar content in the forward-aged order backlog is healthy and growing. Another turnaround management philosopher, Mae West, once said, "I've been rich and I've been poor. Rich is better." There are only two types of problems that management ever faces: growth is one, liquidation is the other. Growth problems are better.

When the total margin dollars have flattened or dropped, you want to bring volume back up, of course. "Reduce prices" sound good? That's about all, it only *sounds* good. You do *not* reduce posted or list price. You *do* increase discounts from those prices because of "volume/cost considerations."

If the majority of your firm's sales normally result from a bidding process, here are a few useful insights. If you're in a Stage 1, get out a sharp pencil. You *must* get the volume. Don't merely low-ball, however. Get approval for a bid modification with regard to pay terms. Submit a bid significantly lower than what your best guess is of what the competition will bid, but "justify" the disparity by receipt of as much money as you can get with receipt of order—never less than, say, 50 percent. I've been in situations where getting 75–80 percent was achieved.

If you're facing a stage later than Stage 1, consider the follow-on parts supply business potential and the post-sale installation support proximity. The greater the follow-on parts business potential, the *lower* the bid price can be. The closer the installation site, the *lower* the bid price can be. Of course, the more that you are able to exert a favorable influence on product specifications, the *higher* the bid price can be irrespective of either follow-on business or proximity.

### 26. Increase Cash Discounts

In a way, this is a variation of price reduction. The flipside is that you get more cash quicker than you otherwise would have. This is, principally, a Stage 1 action. It's less valuable as you reach later stages; *unless* you use it as a means to lower price after total margin dollars in forward-aged order backlog has flattened or eroded somewhat.

The aims are to increase volume, move otherwise nonliquid inventory, and telescope the billing-to-cash receipt cycle. With regard to increasing volume, recall that if you're in Stage 1, you really don't care if you "steal" some volume from the future. The basic idea is to give the firm a future. Converting slow-moving inventory to cash quickly is always a good move.

### 27. Loosen Credit Criteria

A frequently encountered source of super-false management pride is the report that shows that the firm has experienced a zero percent bad debt expense! Why false pride? Well, an abnormally low bad debt expense is only another way of saying that the firm has not optimized or even maximized sales revenue.

Bad debt expense is like ice cream or booze. A "little" is great but "too much" will kill you. How much is "too much"? That depends, of course on the condition of the firm's financial health, just as the corresponding amounts of ice cream and booze depend upon the individual's physical health.

How much should credit criteria be loosened? Well, if you're in Stage 1 and if there is considerable inventory that can be converted into shippable product with minimal additional cash outlays, then first calculate the approximate (Macro-Tool M2) sales volume that can be generated by the on-hand inventory. Then, begin to loosen credit notch by notch until either the identified sales volume is reached or the criteria have reached bare minimum. Remember, it's better to have dollars invested in receivables than in inventory. The closer to cash, the better!

## GET COSTS DOWN!

The final four remedial actions are all more valuable with turnaround stages beyond Stage 1. All four require preparatory steps that consume more time than that demanded by the urgency and immediacy of Stage 1. This is amply illustrated in Action/Turnaround Stage Relevance Charts 28 through 31 in Appendix 6.

Here's the situation. We face the less virulent form of "turnarounditis"; we face Stages 2, 3, and 4. The firm is usually profitable, but not profitable enough. Cash flow is usually OK, but neither strong nor deep enough. The owners are serious about staying in the business for the "long run." Given these circumstances, the first P, people, is usually OK. Not outstanding, mind you, but certainly OK. There are only two P's left for significant improvement, product and plant. Fortuitously enough, two of the following four actions relate to product and the other two relate to plant.

This is a very important series of actions because we now, finally, deal with improvement of gross margin by cost reduction. Recall where we've been. We started out by trying to stop the bleeding. Then, we moved our focus to expense reduction—mostly "below the gross margin line." Then, we talked about simply removing unprofitable products, customers, and so on. But now we've come to the point where, with the Stage 1 crisis behind us, we can lay the foundation for sound, sustained growth of profitable margin. The implementation of these actions will have profound, truly strategic and enduring impact on the firm. The effects of almost all of the other twenty-seven actions are, by and large, tactical and not particularly long lasting.

## 28. Reduce Labor Cost

Keep in mind that what we're really trying to do is reduce the amount of time that it takes for direct labor personnel to produce the product. Fewer direct labor hours per unit of product—that's our goal. That's the only sure way to reduce labor cost.

There are only two principal approaches. First, change the way the product is made to wring out direct labor time. Second, *redesign* the product such that it takes less time than before to make each unit. Investments and project gestation periods are required for both approaches. To reiterate: in the first approach we leave the product as is but change the work environment, while in the second approach we leave the work environment alone but change the product so that it's easier to produce.

Changing the way that the product is made usually requires significant doses of cash and both manufacturing and industrial engineering. We're dealing with modifications of work stations, plant layout, automation, and the like. Perhaps the most dramatic example of the results that can be obtained with this action is found in the automobile industry, where the growing number of robots has received so much recent publicity.

Product redesign, on the other hand, focuses on changing the product so that less direct labor time is required to produce it. Product redesign consumes considerable R&D, design, and manufacturing engineering expense, but generally little expense is incurred to alter the production environment. This alternative usually takes far more time to implement than the first alternative. The basic reason for this difference is that redesigned prototypes and preproduction models must pass muster in the market place. In-use testing is usually lengthy because the firm and its customers must be assured that the redesigned product meets or exceeds the "old" product performance specifications.

## 29. Reduce Material Cost

The goal of material cost reduction, while it can be simply stated, is really not all that easy to achieve. The cost of material embodied in the product usually in the range of 40–60 percent of the total cost of the product. Thus, even though cost reduction may not be particularly easy, it certainly warrants a vigorous attempt.

How do you start? The very best approach that I know of goes like this. (By the way, if you know of a better approach, please let me know about it, OK?) First, forget about "products." Yep, that's what I said—forget about the finished product that you ship to market. You'll get absolutely nowhere if you start out that way.

Rather, think in terms of *parts*. Products, after all, are nothing more than an accumulation of parts. You incur material costs at the "part" level; don't ever try to reduce material costs at any other level. A faddish label for this concept is "cash inflow/outflow symmetry." You simply cannot reduce either costs or expenses in any way other than in the same manner in which they are incurred. So, OK, you're thinking "parts." But which parts?

Certainly not all parts. Employ the concept of Macro-Tool M5; namely, look for Pareto's law once again. Don't be hesitant, you'll find it sure enough—some 20 percent of the parts will account for about approximately 80 percent of the total cost (see Macro-Tool M2). Have an analysis prepared in descending sequence by part *usage/cost*. It is calculated as follows. Multiply the part's usage by its unit cost to arrive at its usage/cost. Then, sort the results of that calculation in descending order by usage/cost dollars. Show the percentage of the total usage/cost that each part usage/cost represents. Also show a running, cumulative percentage total that will quickly direct you to the array of parts that constitute, say, 80 percent of the total usage cost. You will find cases where only a hundred or fewer parts constitute 80 percent of the total usage/cost of several thousand parts. Not many situations are that badly skewed.

Now, armed with the relatively short list of critical parts, you march down the list asking a series of questions about each of the parts in turn. The answers are usually developed by making personal action assignments to the relevant operational personnel. The first question is, "Do we make or buy this part?" Let's explore the "buy" answer first. Four questions should then be posed and answered. (1) Can we make the part at less cost than the purchase cost? (2) Can we buy the part at a lower cost? (3) Can we convert to a less costly substitute material? (4) Can product redesign remove the part, lessen the quantity needed of the part, or provide opportunity for the use of less costly substitute materials?

If the initial answer is that we make the part, only three questions ensue. (1) Can we buy the part at less cost? (2) Can the cost of the part be reduced by reduction of the cost of the raw material from which it is fabricated? (3) Can the cost of labor to produce the part be reduced? (See Remedial Action 28.)

All of the "yes" answers except one lead you to a relatively lengthy implementation period. The one "yes" that can be quickly implemented is the answer to the question, "Can we buy the part at less cost?" The key premises to implementation of such an action are (1) there is no erosion of material quality or the vendor's service and (2) there is no inventory build resulting from merely purchasing in larger, unusable quantities; you know, the "cheaper by the carload" bargains.

All of the other "yes" answers lead to potential changes in product performance. The "bottom line," just as noted in Action 28 above, the firm and its customers must be assured that changes in material or in production processes/methods do not adversely affect product performance.

## 30. Reduce Capacity

This is the only one of the four actions in this series that does not increase in value the farther one goes into the future. See Action/Turnaround Stage Relevance Chart 30. In Appendix 6. But it does favorably mitigate the problems associated with Stages 2 and 3. Basically, this is a defensive action; your aim is to mitigate downside consequences rather than create and exploit upside opportunities.

The situation is typically this: Sales are falling (Symptom 9), unit sales are declining (Symptom 27), and capacity utilization is decreasing (Symptom 25). Macro-Tool M12 tells us that the forward-aged margin dollar content in order backlog is falling, not so much from margin erosion (Symptom 10) but principally because of unit volume deterioration. Further, the prospects for getting sales up (Actions 26 and 27) range from poor to lousy. We just have to cut back until or unless we have a better alternative. How do we proceed? What do we do?

Start by reviewing Macro-Tools M1 through M8 and M12, and Micro-Tools m1, m2, m3, m17, m18, m19, m20, m31, and m32. Then, armed with these insights and evaluations, proceed through the plant on a department-by-department basis. A manufacturing plant is not one big homogeneous mass; one cannot just, say, sell 30 percent of the plant and thereby reduce capacity costs by 30 percent. A manufacturing plant consists of discrete investment and activity units, but the most important basic differentiation is that between fabrication and assembly. That is, identify those departments that *make* parts (punch press department, screw machine department, die-casting department, and so on) and those departments that *assemble* the parts into subassemblies and finished goods.

As discussed earlier in Section 1, there are only three actions that can be taken. The department's capacity can be (1) consolidated into another department, (2) closed down temporarily, or (3) closed down permanently and/or sold. First, let's discuss the action alternatives with respect to fabrication departments. Consolidation with other departments is almost always infeasible because of the incompatibility of the equipment operation, function, purpose, and use. Fabrication departments, however, usually can be temporarily closed down relatively easily and inexpensively. Closing the department and selling the equipment can realize some near-term cash. However, the amount of cash realized will most probably be below book value (necessitating a charge against the income statement) and it will invariably be less than replacement value. Thus, this action should be avoided unless one or the other of these circumstances prevail: (1) the firm is prepared to permanently, in effect, commit to the purchase of parts now made in those departments, or (2) the decision has been made to eliminate the products that utilize the parts made in those departments.

With respect to assembly departments, consolidation is indeed a viable option. Practicality of consolidation diminishes as the need for special purpose jigs, dies, fixtures increases. And vice versa. Temporary closing is easily implemented. Usually only minimal equipment and facilities maintenance is required. Close-down and sale of fixtures, benches, and the like will generate only trival cash. This step may be easy to implement, but there is no meaningful advantage over merely closing the department temporarily.

In terms of the entire plant, unless the firm is a relatively large multiplant operation, sale of the plant is equivalent to liquidation—evidence of the failure of the turnaround.

## 31. Increase Capacity Utilization

Sure! But how? We're in a turnaround, we've got excess capacity and probably will have it in the foreseeable future. Sales in our business are relatively flat or they're certainly not growing fast enough to tax our present capacity. Aha! Therein lies the heart of this remedial action. Don't limit your operational capacity strategies only to your "basic" business! Get involved quickly in "marginal business." Just what is marginal business? Essentially it means producing goods that are sold at price levels which just cover or are slightly in excess of the cost of production.

The basic aim of this business is to improve profit and cash flow at the factory or plant level by excess coverage of "fixed" and perhaps even "variable" burden expenses.

Keep the pursuit of marginal business as far as possible from the served markets of your basic business. Why? Because you'll screw up the markets on which you must ultimately and fundamentally depend if you fail to keep it separate. Your firm could become known as a "price-cutter." You'll cause intolerable static in your firm's communications with distributors, customers, reps, and so on. You'll contaminate the firm's "pipeline" to the market.

Be sure, also, to keep in mind that we're *not* talking about marginal *products*. Usually, that term refers to products whose performance or quality is unreliable or otherwise suspect. OK, we're not talking about the firm's basic business and we're not talking about marginal products. What the hell *are* we talking about, then? Well, the following dozen characteristics should explain a great deal.

*The Less Assembly the Better*

Ideal marginal business involves only fabrication. That way equipment utilization is favored. Assembly requires training and complicates quality control because functional specifications must be met in addition to dimensional specifications. Fabricating parts is the kind of business you want.

*The Less the Engineering Content the Better*

What you should be looking for are simple, uncomplicated parts. You want to avoid investment in costly, complex dies or molds. You're looking to process standard raw materials. Avoid titanium, beryllium, and the like. Good old one-and-a-half-inch machining rod is always a winner. The more standardized or transferable the raw material, the better.

*Components Are Better Than Finished Goods*

This is another way of saying that fabricating parts that are alien and unconnected to your basic business are most desirable as marginal business. Finished goods production complicates quality control and always raises warranty and product liability issues that can and should be avoided. The last thing you need when facing a turnaround is a whole new batch of product service problems with a product that is unfamiliar to your personnel!

## *Direct, OEM Sales Force*

Because your primary focus should be on piece parts or components, the most effective sales channel goes directly from your firm to the manufacturer-customer. Marketing expense should be low; you really don't need slick ads or promo material. Above all, don't try to use your existing sales force or channels. Not only won't they be very good at it, they will also be exposed to cut-rate pricing. The practice may even be carried over by them into your basic business. Manufacturers' Reps are usually a good channel. But there's an even better one. Seek out "retired" purchasing agents of large manufacturers. They know the inner workings of your prospective customers and can quickly showcase your capabilities to the "right" people.

## *The Faster the Turnaround Cycle the Better*

The kind of turn-around we're talking about here is production cycle time. In other words, the more that the firm's basic business raw materials are used, the better. The shorter the time period between order receipt and shipment, the better. You want to get the order, pump out the parts, ship and collect the cash as quickly as possible.

## Segregation Accounting

If you're going after marginal business, don't let the numbers get mixed up. Set up the appropriate accounts and subaccounts such that you can quickly and relatively accurately assess status and prognosis.

## Cash on the Barrelhead

Because your price for manufacturing components and parts will be dramatically lower than that otherwise available to the customer, it is relatively easy to negotiate favorable pay terms—very favorable pay terms. It is possible to obtain partial payment upon receipt of the order. In *no* case should "standard" terms be accepted.

## Raw Material Inventory—PERIOD

With the aggressive pricing that marginal business requires, you simply cannot afford to maintain inventory at subassembly and/or finished goods levels. This is yet another way of focusing on parts or components devoid of follow-on assembly operations.

## Plus or Minus One-Quarter of an Inch

The point here is that you must avoid ultra-precision, light-beam tolerance types of fabrication *unless* of course you happen to have the equipment to handle it. Otherwise, all you're doing is asking for truly significant problems. Yes, the volume may look attractive. Yes, your independent rep may have given you all the appropriate assurances. After all, his commission is at stake. Yes, sometimes even your own operations personnel tell you that they're confident they can (somehow) handle it. Best advice? *Don't take any marginal business unless it's beneath your present operational levels of performance and capability.* Stretch your organizational competence, instead, in your basic business. It will have more enduring value and more certainty.

*Flexible Delivery*

During order negotiations and, again, because of the extremely favorable price that you are offering, obtain a flexible delivery schedule. In other words, you want to produce the parts for the customer somewhat at your convenience and not "under the gun" to meet a tight schedule. You do not want to foul up the production schedule for your basic business. You do want to fit in the marginal business around and in between performance of your basic business.

*Plain Brown Wrapper*

Ideally, what you want to do is pump out the parts ordered, throw them in a big box and ship bulk-packed. The last thing you want to do is invest big bucks in specially designed, customized shipping containers. Not only because they're costly but also because they are predicated on a fragility of the parts that you want no responsibility for.

*Focus on Operations—NOT Market*

Your primary and virtually exclusive goal is to maximize utilization of your expensive and costly fabrication equipment. You will make more profit as more machine hours are logged. Your aim is not to enter new markets. Certainly not at these prices and margins! Always view involvement in marginal business as temporary operational work load until you can replace that equipment usage with more (really much more) profitable products to meet the needs of your basic served markets. How much marginal business should you shoot for? See Micro-Tool, m32 above. The difference between anticipated capacity utilization and 100 percent utilization measures the capacity "gap" available for marginal business.

# SECTION VI

# THE OPERATING ORGANIZATION—KEY TO TURNAROUND SUCCESS

### Overview

You should be asking why the final section of this *Handbook* is not entitled, "The Turnaround Plan" or something similar rather than "The Operating Organization." Most other so-called management books do indeed cap their expositions with something akin to the former title. That's because the authors miss the point! No surprise. Most of them have never run a company. Their misplaced focus bespeaks their bureaucratic staff mentality—they're more interested in "filling out the forms properly" than seeing to it that the "right" action is taken. They display their ignorance of the primacy of *people*. They tout only the process.

*People* are always the firm's most important and potent asset. If you have excellent product and excellent plant, but only mediocre people, the results will predictably be only mediocre. Conversely, give me mediocre product and mediocre plant but excellent people and you can bet that results will sure as hell be excellent.

No plan is ever "perfect." No matter how hard you try, there will be errors of both omission and commission. Correction of these errors can only be made by people. The more competent these people are, the more quickly and fully will those errors be erased.

The enthusiasm with which people try to implement any plan, the more likely that the execution will be better, more complete. The greater the enthusiasm (or morale, if you prefer), the more performance will reflect the spirit of the plan, and the less performance will be compliance only to the letter. Never forget that everyone can conceptualize, but only a few, rare people *can* and *do* get the job done.

So, while this section does include discussion of turnaround plan formulation, keep in mind the entire time that mobilizing the firm's operational organization and creating an environment for vigorous "stretch" performance is of paramount importance. Therefore, the organizational mobilization process should begin even as the turnaround plan is being formulated. You cannot rouse people with ho-hum minutiae. So, make no little plans—they have no magic to stir men's blood.

There is no need to shy away from making big, ambitious, aggressive plans. Most people don't because they fear failure. Only 3 percent of all people are "winners" and even those 3 percent "fail" 49 percent of the time. They are winners nonetheless because their 51 percent success rate achieves overwhelmingly more than the "play-it-safers" do. It is impossible to reach second base if you insist on keeping one foot on first.

Your turnaround plan should be vibrant, dynamic, compelling, aggressive, attention-getting, even inspirational—but most important it must be do-able! The plan itself is the basic, fundamental motivational opportunity. It should not be a cold, dispassionate, esoteric collection of dry, sterile financial statements and exhibits. Rather, it should be challenging, personal, easy to comprehend, and easy to monitor. It should pinpoint and spotlight personal assignments and commitments. People will react to, act on, respond to and believe in only what they either fear or desire. The plan should encourage their desire for job security, career enhancement, and a brighter future. Never play on their fear.

Your entire turnaround effort, including the plan, should be governed by only one overriding priority. All of your actions, appearances, conversations, and meetings should give preeminence to "doing the right thing" rather than only "doing things right." It's far, far better to do 95 percent of the right thing than to meticulously complete 100 percent of something that may not be wrong, but just isn't right.

## THE TURNAROUND PLAN

A turnaround plan is, first and foremost, a plan. What are some of the key hallmarks of planning? For a thorough discussion, see *No-Nonsense Planning* (Macmillan, 1984). The following are some of the more important highlights.

What *is* planning? It is the process of deciding what to change today so that tomorrow will be significantly different from yesterday. Note that planning is a series of decisions about what *to do;* NOT the doing itself. Planning is an exercise in anticipation. It requires the ability to foresee likely consequences of prior, yet untaken action. It is the ability, too, to forge an inference chain backwards from a desired future result to the present set of circumstances. The chain is always forged backwards because a basic law of planning is, "Never depart from the previous until the way is paved for the subsequent."

There are three basic turnaround plan sections. They are the target forecast, the run-rate forecast, and the objective forecast. As discussed earlier, the target forecast embodies the minimum financial performance levels of the firm that will sufficiently mollify the owners/creditors such that they will refrain from disinvestment or foreclosure action. The run-rate forecast is a projection of financial performance of the firm if *no* changes are implemented by operating management; essentially, it is a measure of the "do nothing new" alternative. The objective forecast, in effect, is the numerical difference between the earlier two forecasts. The objective forecast identifies the specific line-items on the P&L, balance sheet, and cash flow, and measurably defines the magnitudes of the changes in the firm's performance which the operating management must meet or exceed. Each of these forecasts is formatted in the traditional statements: cash (funds) flow, income statement, and balance sheet.

The core of the turnaround plan is the objective forecast. The target and run-rate forecasts are used almost exclusively as the parametric means to identify and quantify the tasks required to achieve turnaround success. Your job, essentially, is to assign to the "right" people the remedial, restorative actions which you have selected after employment of the analytical tools to properly evaluate the symptoms. Duck soup, huh?

For example, let's say you've got to get cash flow up from "here" to "there." There is no way that it all can be done in one fell swoop. Rather, you should build the action bridge from "here" to "there" with a number of actions. View the actions as bricks. Usually, the smaller they are, the better—they're easier to understand and manage, and you can then afford failure of some of them without bringing down the whole bridge.

In the core of your turnaround plan is the objective forecast; the heart of that core is the future twelve-month calendarized, cumulative effect of the selected actions; the action assignment calendar (refer to the beginning of Section V to refresh your recollection). Each one of those calendar entries should represent a specific action assignment to a specific person in the operating organization. And, obviously, it is the cumulative and combinative effect of the results of these action assignments that will enable the firm to meet or exceed the target forecast; that will result in a successful turnaround.

## HOW TO MOTIVATE AND MONITOR THE OPERATING ORGANIZATION

Motivating employees is really not all that difficult or mysterious. By and large, people simply want to know: (1) what's expected of them, (2) where they stand, (3) how they can progress in their job and career, and (4) how they can make more money. Sometimes one individual or another holds them in different priority. Personally, I prefer the relatively easy task of motivating people who are primarily interested in how they can make more money. Remember, it is most unlikely that the firm got into trouble because the majority of the incumbent personnel continually fouled things up. You will find, almost universally, that the majority of the incumbents really and truly want to do a good job and be recognized for it, irrespective of sex, race, religion, or national origin.

Of invaluable help in breaking the management tasks into manageable quanta is the Analysis of Change In Operating Pre-Tax (Figure 4). The focus on change of pre-tax is not misplaced. You will find that as the target forecast is being formulated, the attention and concern of the owners/creditors is riveted to the "bottom line." In turnaround Stages 1 and probably 2, principal focus will be on cash generation rather than profit. But consideration of operating profit can never be ignored and in Stages 3 and 4 it is of paramount importance.

The anticipated results of each of the selected remedial actions should be traced to each quantitative change in pre-tax posted on Figure 4. Thus, looking ahead to the plan communication sessions, Figure 4 becomes the centerpiece and, in conjunction with the action assignment calendar, the audience—whether owners, creditors, customers, vendors, employees, or operating management—can be led, small step by small step, along the firm's planned recovery route. Credibility of your plan and acceptance of it will zoom as the magnitude of each recovery step diminishes. The audience will universally be looking for downside exposure; some may even tend to view the glass not only as half-empty, but cracked as well. By obviating the need for the audience to make too large an inferential leap, you not only enhance acceptance, you generate confidence in the plan's ultimate success. In sum, you will use Figure 4 not only for monitoring control, but for building credibility and monitoring operational management performance as well.

Figure 4 is designed for firms that manufacture and sell products, but similar ones can be (and have been) developed for service firms. The lines 1 through 23 display a typical or traditional income statement format. The columns A and W are used to record the run-rate forecast and target forecast, respectively. Columns B through V are used to show the respective line-item pre-tax changes which lead from run-rate forecast to target forecast. Support forms should be used to further highlight the changes in operating pre-tax in the "below the line" expense cate-

**Figure 4.** (*Pages 194–195*): Analysis of Change in Operating Pre-Tax

Adapted from Richard S. Sloma, *No-Nonsense Planning* (New York: The Free Press), pp. 110–111. Copyright © 1984 by The Free Press.

|  | | | SALES | | | LABOR COST INCREASE | | LABOR COST REDUCTION | | MATERIAL PRICE | |
|---|---|---|---|---|---|---|---|---|---|---|---|
|  | RUN-RATE FORECAST | VOLUME | MIX | PRICE | POPULATION | WAGES | POPULATION | WAGES | MIX | INCREASE | COST REDUCTION |
|  | A | B | C | D | E | F | G | H | I | J | K |
| 1. Gross Sales | | | | | | | | | | | |
| 2. Returns and Allowances | | | | | | | | | | | |
| 3. Net Sales | | | | | | | | | | | |
| 4. Commissions | | | | | | | | | | | |
| 5. NAC Sales | | | | | | | | | | | |
| 6. Standard Cost of Sales | | | | | | | | | | | |
| 7. Standard Margin | | | | | | | | | | | |
| 8. Labor Variance | | | | | | | | | | | |
| 9. Material Variance | | | | | | | | | | | |
| 10. Burden Variance | | | | | | | | | | | |
| 11. Gross Margin | | | | | | | | | | | |
| 12. Obsolescence | | | | | | | | | | | |
| 13. Warranty | | | | | | | | | | | |
| 14. Total Cost of Sales | | | | | | | | | | | |
| 15. Net Return on Sales | | | | | | | | | | | |
| 16. Operations Management | | | | | | | | | | | |
| 17. Engineering In-House | | | | | | | | | | | |
| 18. Engineering Contract | | | | | | | | | | | |
| 19. Total Engineering | | | | | | | | | | | |
| 20. Selling Expense | | | | | | | | | | | |
| 21. Adminstrative Expense | | | | | | | | | | | |
| 22. Total "Below the Line" | | | | | | | | | | | |
| 23. Operating Pre-tax | | | | | | | | | | | |

|  | | BURDEN | | | | | | | | | |
|  | | COST INCREASES | | | COST REDUCTION | | | BELOW THE LINE EXPENSES | | | |
| POPULATION | WAGES | OTHER EXPENSES | POPULATION | WAGES | OTHER EXPENSES | OPERATIONS | MANAGEMENT | ENGINEERING | SELLING | ADMINISTRATIVE | OBJECTIVE FORECAST | TARGET FORECAST |
| L. | M | N | O | P | Q | R | S | T | U | V | W |

gories; such as operations management, engineering, sales (or distribution), and general/administrative. In some firms, operations management may be included in the burden pool. Nonetheless, it is useful for planning purposes to highlight this ofttimes significant expense to avoid losing actual expense control while exploring the "absorption effect" measurement. Also, it is useful for planning purposes to highlight (also for control purposes) the total expenses, however reclassified.

First of all, be mindful that even with the most thorough and complete utilization, many of the intersectional cells will be blanks. In other words, don't allow your subordinates to be overawed by the mere appearance of the form (of course, *you* won't). This is *not* a "government" form, where it is required that all of the blanks must be filled in.

Second, note that it is *not* an accounting form. It is aimed at communication at the management level. It provides for a blend of traditional accounting system data with non-accounting system data treatment, such as population levels and the ground rule that parentheses *always* means UNFAVORABLE (all together now: hooray! from those of us who always have trouble keeping it straight!).

Third, it is *not* a "magic" form. It is only one version of what you should refine or tailor to suit the needs of your particular firm. Nor will filling it out and filing it away result in objective achievement. It *is,* after all, only a tool. And how you, as the craftsman, *use* that tool will really determine what the end results will be.

Tie in the quantitative intersectional cell data, first, to an incentive compensation plan (objective not subjective, measurable, etc.—all that good stuff), and secondly, to the weekly management report. OK, it's time to start walking through the form to make sure that we really understand it. Let's begin with the column headings.

## THE COLUMNS

### 1. Effect of Sales on Pre-Tax

Columns B, C, and D present, respectively, the planned *changes* (both favorable and unfavorable) from run-rate forecast, in volume, mix, and price. Thus, direct measurable clarity is focused on what otherwise is, at best, a "fuzzy" number. Volume and mix projections can be interrogated back into the supporting plans for order intake which, in turn, can be further traced into the supporting sales promotion and new product plans to insure harmony and consistency both in timing and dollars.

Targeting a specific price effect provides managerial audit of the pricing program to insure timing and adequacy of amount of increase. This, in turn, will insure capture, so that the planned pre-tax contribution is achieved.

### 2. Effect of Manufacturing Cost on Pre-Tax

Columns E through Q provide for display of specifics relative to objective plan behavior of the three prime cost elements: labor, material, and burden. First, labor—columns E, F, G, and H. The pattern of analysis for both labor and burden as we shall see later is the same; namely, first the identification of those elements that *increase* cost, then identification of cost reduction goals to *offset* the cost increases. First the "bad news"; then, the "good news." For labor analysis, both population and wages are shown. Thus, inferences can be quantified relative to average wages paid and effect on efficiency (by cross-reference to line 8, *Labor Variance*); insight is gained into the burden absorption base (cross-referencing population with line 10, *Burden Variance,* and labor efficiency levels identified earlier), and so on. Similarly, the aggressiveness of planned cost reduction is more visible by study of columns G and H, both in absolute terms and in comparative or relative terms by cross-reference to population percent changes which are affected by cost reduction, and so on.

The key determinants of material cost are mix (column I) and price (columns J and K). In each of these instances, quantified projections are required to show both the unfavorable *and* the favorable budgeted performances.

Burden cost (columns L through Q) is analyzed again from both the "increases" and "expense reduction" viewpoints; again relating population levels to expense levels. Columns N and Q, "Other Expenses" are *not* meant to mean "miscellaneous"; they include all expenses not directly related to population. The numbers can be quite large.

3. **Effect of "Below the Line" Expenses on Pre-Tax**

Columns R through U present both the favorable and unfavorable effects on planned performance. In each case, population levels must be related to dollar expense levels for managerial "reasonability testing."

Column V is used to display the summed changes recorded in Columns B through U and represents the planned quantum performance improvement over the run-rate forecast; it embodies the objective forecast. Column W is derived by combining columns A and V.

## THE LINES

Now, let's proceed *down* the Income Statement, line by line. Lines 1 through 5 deal exclusively with *sales. Returns and Allowances,* and *Commissions* are deducted from *Gross Sales* to arrive at *Net After Commission (NAC)* sales. They interface with Columns B, C and D.

Lines 6 through 10 evaluate cost and goods sold so that, by subtraction, line 11, the *Gross Margin,* is generated. Figure 4 is designed to accommodate a standard cost system. If you use another costing method, merely substitute the appropriate lines. Inferences drawn from intersectional entries on the "variance" lines (8, 9, and 10) are particularly useful. Insight into the planned changes, for example, in labor efficiency can be gained by study of the entries in the labor variance/population (or line 8/column G) intersection.

Given steady or rising volume (column B), decreases in population should improve labor variance, or at least reduce the adverse effect of increased wages (column F).

Line 11, *Gross Margin,* is sometimes called "factory profit." To obtain *Total Cost of Sales* (or "cost of goods sold"), provision for *Obsolescence* (line 12) and *Warranty* (line 13) costs are subtracted from *Gross Margin* (line 11).

The *Net Return on Sales* (line 15) shows the gross profit available to cover operating expenses and operating pre-tax.

Lines 16 through 21 show planned behavior of the "below the line" expenses. Line 16, *Operations Management,* assumes that production control/scheduling purchasing, industrial or manufacturing engineering, and so on are treated as period or line-item expenses. This simply means that they are not included in the burden pool and thus are not incorporated into inventory via burden absorption. This is probably the most conservative treatment. It keeps these expenses out of the balance sheet and retains them in the income statement. It tends to reduce reported operating pre-tax, particularly if volume is sufficiently high to permit overabsorption.

Lines 17 and 18 provide means to analyze engineering expense from both the in-house and contract viewpoints. *Selling Expense* (line 20) includes marketing, advertising, promotion, shows, conventions, and so on, as well as direct selling expenses.

*Administrative Expense* (line 21) includes the usual assortment of accounting, finance, administrative, accrual, interest and other expenses. Line 22 (*Total "Below the Line"*) is the sum of lines 16 through 21 and it is subtracted from line 15 (*Net Return on Sales*) to arrive finally at *Operating Pre-Tax.*

Following the steps in this *Handbook* will insure the creation of just the kind of work environment that is most conducive to employee motivation. And, the analysis of change in operating pre-tax (Figure 4), coupled with the calendarized assigned results (the action assignment calendar) are the raw material with which a meaningful incentive compensation program (ICP) can be constructed. Figure 4 spells out *what* needs to be done, while the action assignment calendar spells out *when* those results must be achieved. And both are tied to *who* is responsible to see to it that it's done.

In a turnaround situation, if you really want to be successful, forget all about the oft-quoted maxim, "If you do a really good job you get to keep it." Application of that approach simply will not get the job done. In a turnaround, you have to get better performance from the people than they themselves sometimes feel they can deliver.

The best way to approach the motivational aspect of your job is to get the understanding across that salary and tenure is dependent upon meeting the objective forecast. Not in every respect or detail, mind you, but in total. If the objective is to improve dynamic margin by $100, with $60 coming from price increase and $40 coming from expense reduction, you (and the owners/creditors) really shouldn't care if the actual results show $40 from price increase and $60 from expense reduction, so long as the total is still $100 *and* the firm is not fatally crippled from excessive expense cuts.

Even when facing a Stage 1 cash crunch, offer meaningful amounts of ICP (incentive compensation) for achievement (1) in excess of the objective forecast and/or (2) significantly sooner than that called for in the objective forecast and the action assignment calendar. If actual performance surpasses required performance, the firm can very well afford to share the excess with the overachievers. A professionally thought-out ICP, founded on the objective forecast, the analysis of change of operating pre-tax (Figure 4), and the action assignment calendar, *will* meet all four motivational criteria.

First, the objective forecast, the analysis of change of operating pre-tax, and the action assignment calendar let the assignees and subordinates know *exactly* what is expected of them *and* when it is expected. Second, with weekly reporting of actual performance compared to objective performance, each assignee and subordinate knows *exactly* where he or she stands, without having to be told. Besides, if the weekly status report of all assignments is distributed to everyone who submits one, office "politics" is held to a bare minimum. It's terribly hard, after all, to be devious in a fishbowl!

Third, it's pretty clear that the extent to which each employee meets or exceeds the quantified, impersonal goals in the objective forecast, the analysis of change of operating pre-tax, and the action assignment calendar is a direct indication of prospects for progress in the job or career. Finally, the degree to which the objective forecast, analysis of change of operating pre-tax, and the action assignment calendar goals are exceeded should readily be calculable into dollars and cents by each participant in the incentive compensation program.

Operational personnel can, if the ICP is documented and published throughout the organization, rest assured that they are not tainted by the prior financial performance of the firm. Sure, there will come a time when you have to remove incumbents; but, rather than removal based on some version of subjective prejudice, the decision will hinge on measurable and impersonal performance results. And that's the way it really ought to be! *Never judge people—only measure and evaluate results and performance.* Easy to say, isn't it? But most people simply can't or won't do it in that professional way. Well, I guess that's only another way of saying that "most people" will never be successful turnaround managers.

But if you really put this *Handbook* into practice, you know that *you will be successful.* Good luck (sometimes that does enter into it) and drop me a line to let me know how you're doing.

# APPENDIX 1

# COMPLETE CATALOG OF KEY SYMPTOMS

*(See pages 42–67)*

1. Inability to Pay Debt Service
2. Inability to Pay "Taxes"
3. Inability to Pay Contractual Obligations
4. Inability to Pay Accounts Payable
5. Inability to Pay Salaries, Wages, Commissions
6. Inability to Pay Fringes, Pensions, Etc.
7. Inability to Pay Purchase Commitments
8. Excessive Debt/Equity Ratio
9. Flat, Falling Sales
10. Eroding Gross Margin
11. Increasing Unit Labor Cost
12. Increasing Unit Material Cost
13. Increasing Burden: People-Related Variable Expense
14. Increasing Burden: People-Related Fixed Expense
15. Increasing Burden: Plant-Related Variable Expense
16. Increasing Burden: Plant-Related Fixed Expense
17. Increasing Sales/Marketing Expense
18. Increasing Finance/Administration Expense

19. Increasing Engineering In-House People-Related Expense
20. Increasing Engineering Contract People-Related Expense
21. Increasing Engineering In-House Product-Related Expense
22. Increasing Engineering Contract Product-Related Expense
23. Inconsistent Valuation of Inventory Input/Output
24. Increasing Warranty Expense
25. Decreasing Capacity Utilization
26. Decreasing Product Line Profitability
27. Decreasing Unit Sales
28. Decreasing Customer Profitability

# APPENDIX 2

# KIT OF MACRO-TOOLS

(*See pages 72–89*)

M1. Financial Statements
M2. The Art of Approximation
M3. The Turnaround Plan
M4. Sanity Checks
M5. Subaccount Analysis
M6. Pre-Tax Return on Sales
M7. Pre-Tax Return on Assets
M8. Pre-Tax Return on Equity
M9. Profitability of Marketing/Sales Channels
M10. Profitability of Marketing/Sales Region
M11. Profitability of Marketing/Sales Representative
M12. Forward-Aged Margin Dollar Content in Order Backlog

# APPENDIX 3

# KIT OF MICRO-TOOLS

(*See pages 89–119*)

m1. Product Line Gross Margin Percent Profitability
m2. Product, Model, Catalog Number Gross Margin Percent Profitability
m3. Cumulative Margin $ by Product, Model, Catalog Number
m4. Direct Labor Compensation $ as Percent of Sales
m5. Indirect Labor Compensation $ as Percent of Sales
m6. Customer Gross Margin Percent Profitability
m7. Customer Gross Margin $ Profitability
m8. Cumulative Gross Margin $ by Customer
m9. Cumulative Gross Margin $ by Region
m10. Cumulative Gross Margin $ by Sales/Marketing Channel
m11. Cumulative Gross Margin $ by Representative
m12. Product Line Dynamic Margin Percent Profitability
m13. Product Line Dynamic Margin $ Profitability

m14. Cumulative Dynamic Margin $ by Product Line
m15. Product Material Cost as Percent of Sales
m16. Product Direct Labor Cost as Percent of Sales
m17. Burden People-Related Variable Expense as Percent of Sales
m18. Burden People-Related Fixed Expense as Percent of Sales
m19. Burden Plant-Related Variable Expense as Percent of Sales
m20. Burden Plant-Related Fixed Expense as Percent of Sales
m21. Sales/Marketing People-Related Expense as Percent of Sales
m22. Sales/Marketing Other Expense as Percent of Sales
m23. Finance/Administration People-Related Expense as % of Sales
m24. Finance/Administration Other Expense as Percent of Sales
m25. Engineering In-House People-Related Expense as Percent of Sales
m26. Engineering Contract People-Related Expense as Percent of Sales
m27. Engineering In-House Product-Related Expense as Percent of Sales
m28. Engineering Contract Product-Related Expense as Percent of Sales
m29. Warranty Expense as Percent of Sales
m30. Sales Dollars per Employee
m31. Sales Dollars per Plant Square Foot
m32. Capacity Utilization Percent

m33. Compensation $ per Direct Labor Employee
m34. Compensation $ per Indirect Labor Employee
m35. Overtime Premium $ per Direct Labor Employee
m36. Overtime Premium $ per Indirect Labor Employee

# APPENDIX 4

# ARSENAL OF REMEDIAL, RESTORATIVE ACTIONS

*"Immediate" Cash Flow Improvement (Pages 136–144)*

1. "Fire-Sale" Inventory
2. Factor Accounts Receivable
3. Renegotiate Union Contracts
4. Renegotiate Credit Lines and Debt Service
5. Renegotiate Vendor Terms
6. Reduce Purchases

*Reduce People-Related Expense (Pages 145–155)*

7. Variable Burden
8. Fixed Burden
9. Sales/Marketing
10. In-House Engineering
11. Contract Engineering
12. Finance/Administration

*Reduce Product-Related Expense (Pages 155–158)*

13. Sales/Marketing
14. In-House Engineering
15. Contract Engineering

*Reduce Plant-Related Expense (Pages 158–161)*

16. Variable Burden
17. Fixed Burden
18. In-House Engineering
19. Contract Engineering

*If It Hurts, Don't Do It! (Pages 161–167)*

20. Eliminate Unprofitable Products
21. Eliminate Unprofitable Customers
22. Eliminate Unprofitable Channels
23. Eliminate Unprofitable Regions
24. Eliminate Unprofitable Reps

*Get Sales UP! (Pages 167–172)*

25. Raise Prices!
26. Increase Cash Discounts
27. Loosen Credit Criteria

*Get Costs DOWN! (Pages 173–185)*

28. Reduce Labor Cost
29. Reduce Material Cost
30. Reduce Capacity
31. Increase Capacity Utilization

# APPENDIX 5

# ACTION/SYMPTOM/ ANALYTICAL TOOL INTERREFERENCE TABLE

| ACTION | SYMPTOMS | MACRO-TOOLS | MICRO-TOOLS |
|---|---|---|---|
| *"Immediate" Cash Flow Improvement* ||||
| 1 | 1–8, 23 | 1, 4, 5, 7 | 1, 2, 15, 29 |
| 2 | 1–8, 28 | 1, 5, 7 | 6–11, 21, 22 |
| 3 | 1–8, 11, 26 | 1, 2, 12 | 3, 4, 5, 16, 33–36 |
| 4 | 1–8 | 1, 3, 5, 12 | 3, 8, 32 |
| 5 | 1–8, 10, 12, 25, 27 | 1, 2, 3, 5, 12 | 3, 15, 32 |
| 6 | 1–9, 25, 27 | 1, 2, 3, 5, 12 | 3, 15, 19, 20, 22, 24, 27, 28 |
| *Reduce People-Related Expense* ||||
| 7 | 5, 6, 13, 17–20 | 1, 2, 5, 12 | 3, 5, 8, 17, 21, 23, 25, 26, 33, 34, 35, 36 |
| 8 | 5, 6, 14, 25, 27 | 1, 2, 5 | 5, 18, 32, 34, 36 |
| 9 | 5, 6, 9, 10, 17, 26, 27, 28 | 1, 2, 5, 9, 10, 11, 12 | 3, 8, 9–14, 21 |
| 10 | 5, 6, 19, 25, 27 | 1, 2, 4, 5, 12 | 1, 2, 3, 25, 29, 32 |
| 11 | 3, 9, 20, 27 | 1, 2, 4, 12 | 26, 29, 32 |
| 12 | 5, 6, 9, 18, 27 | 1, 2, 5, 12 | 3, 8, 23 |

| ACTION | SYMPTOMS | MACRO-TOOLS | MICRO-TOOLS |
|---|---|---|---|
| | *Reduce Product-Related Expense* | | |
| 13 | 10, 15, 16, 24–28 | 2, 3, 4, 5, 9–12 | 1, 2, 3, 6–14, 22 |
| 14 | 10, 21, 24–28 | 2, 3, 4, 5, 12 | 15, 16, 27, 29 |
| 15 | 10, 22, 24–28 | 2, 3, 4, 5, 12 | 15, 16, 28, 29 |
| | *Reduce Plant-Related Expense* | | |
| 16 | 2, 3, 15, 25, 27 | 2, 5, 12 | 19, 31, 32, 34, 36 |
| 17 | 2, 3, 16, 25, 27 | 2, 4, 5, 12 | 20, 31, 32, 34, 36 |
| 18 | 2, 3, 15, 16, 25, 27 | 2, 4, 5, 12 | 19, 20, 25, 31, 32, 34, 36 |
| 19 | 2, 3, 15, 16, 25, 27 | 2, 4, 5, 12 | 19, 20, 26, 31, 32, 34, 36 |
| | *If It Hurts, Don't Do It!* | | |
| 20 | 10, 11, 12, 24, 26, 28 | 2, 4, 12 | 1, 2, 3, 12, 13, 14, 22 |
| 21 | 10, 17, 24, 26, 27, 28 | 2, 4, 12 | 1, 2, 3, 6, 7, 8, 22 |
| 22 | 10, 17, 24, 26, 28 | 2, 4, 9, 12 | 1, 2, 3, 10, 22 |
| 23 | 10, 17, 24, 26, 28 | 2, 4, 10, 12 | 1, 2, 3, 9, 22 |
| 24 | 10, 17, 24, 26, 28 | 2, 4, 11, 12 | 1, 2, 3, 7, 11, 22, 29 |
| | *Get Sales UP!* | | |
| 25 | 9, 10, 25–28 | 1–6, 8, 12 | 1, 2, 3, 8, 30, 31, 32 |
| 26 | 9, 10, 25, 27 | 1, 2, 3, 4, 8, 12 | 1, 2, 3, 8, 30, 31, 32 |
| 27 | 9, 10, 25, 27 | 1, 2, 3, 4, 8, 12 | 1, 2, 3, 8, 9, 10, 11, 24, 29, 30, 31, 32 |
| | *Get Costs DOWN!* | | |
| 28 | 9, 10, 11, 25, 27 | 1, 2, 3, 5–8, 12 | 1, 2, 3, 4, 16, 27, 28, 29 |

| ACTION | SYMPTOMS | MACRO-TOOLS | MICRO-TOOLS |
|---|---|---|---|
| 29 | 9, 10, 12, 25, 27 | 1, 2, 3, 5–8, 12 | 1, 2, 3, 15, 27, 28, 29 |
| 30 | 9, 10, 12, 15, 16, 25, 27 | 1–8, 12 | 1, 2, 3, 17, 18, 19, 20, 31, 32 |
| 31 | 9, 10, 12, 15, 16, 25, 27 | 1–8, 12 | 1, 2, 3, 17, 18, 19, 20, 31, 32 |

# APPENDIX 6

# ACTION/TURNAROUND STAGE RELEVANCE CHARTS

## UNDERSTANDING THE CHARTS

The charts are very easy to interpret. The four vertical "columns" identify each of the four turnaround stages. The height of the curve above the horizontal base line is directly proportional to the action's relevance to each stage. In other words, the closer the curve is to the horizontal base line, the less relevant is that action to that stage.

Also, the greater the height of the curve above the horizontal base line, the greater the favorable effect that the action will generate.

Recall that, in Section V, we saw that the stages occur in lengthening time periods:

Stage 1. Cash Crunch:       NOW!
Stage 2. Cash Shortfall:    3–9 months
Stage 3. Quantity of Profit: 6–12 months
Stage 4. Quality of Profit:  9–18 months

Another insight provided by the charts is the time period needed to implement the action. For example, the Relevance Chart for Action 1, "Fire-Sale" Inventory, shows that the greatest impact is in Stage 1 and that it is easily implemented very quickly. By contrast, the chart for Action 28, Reduce Labor Cost, shows a growingly larger impact stage after stage into the future *and* it shows that reducing labor *cost* cannot be quickly implemented. This is not surprising. Usually, prerequisites to reduction of labor cost include product engineering design changes, manufacturing and industrial engineering work station modification, plant re-layout, acquisition of capital equipment, and so on.

Finally, the shape of the curve is analytically useful. Rather than displaying a constant relevance value for each stage, the curves more realistically reflect the change in relevance value over time. The shape of the curve traces the growing or declining relevance value. Note, for example, the relatively sharply falling relevance value curve for Action 1. At a glance, the curve tells you, correctly, that the action will have its greatest favorable impact early in Stage 1 and that it is virtually irrelevant in Stage 4. That makes sense. If the firm fails to survive the cash crunch, it simply won't be in existence eighteen months from now.

> CAVEAT: *Don't try to read close mathematical precision into these charts. They display relationships; not discrete data.*

## HOW BEST TO USE THE CHARTS

The charts will be of most help if they are frequently scanned, reviewed, pondered and scrutinized. The greater the familiarity that you have with them, the deeper the understanding you will have of the underlying causes and effects. Shoot a copy of them for your briefcase; the next time you're stuck in a delay at the airport or have run out of reading stuff on the plane, thumb through them to refresh your recollection.

A critical time for use of the charts is when the symptoms have begun to crystallize and you begin to define the turnaround stage that you face. Go through them again as you begin selection of remedial actions. Test the validity of your draft (and the final version, too) of your turnaround plan by comparison of action selected to the charts. Use the charts, too, to augment the presentation of your plan to owners, creditors, management, employees and others.

Serious study of these charts and their underlying logic will assure that you do not try to use a cannon to kill a fly and vice versa.

**Action 1**

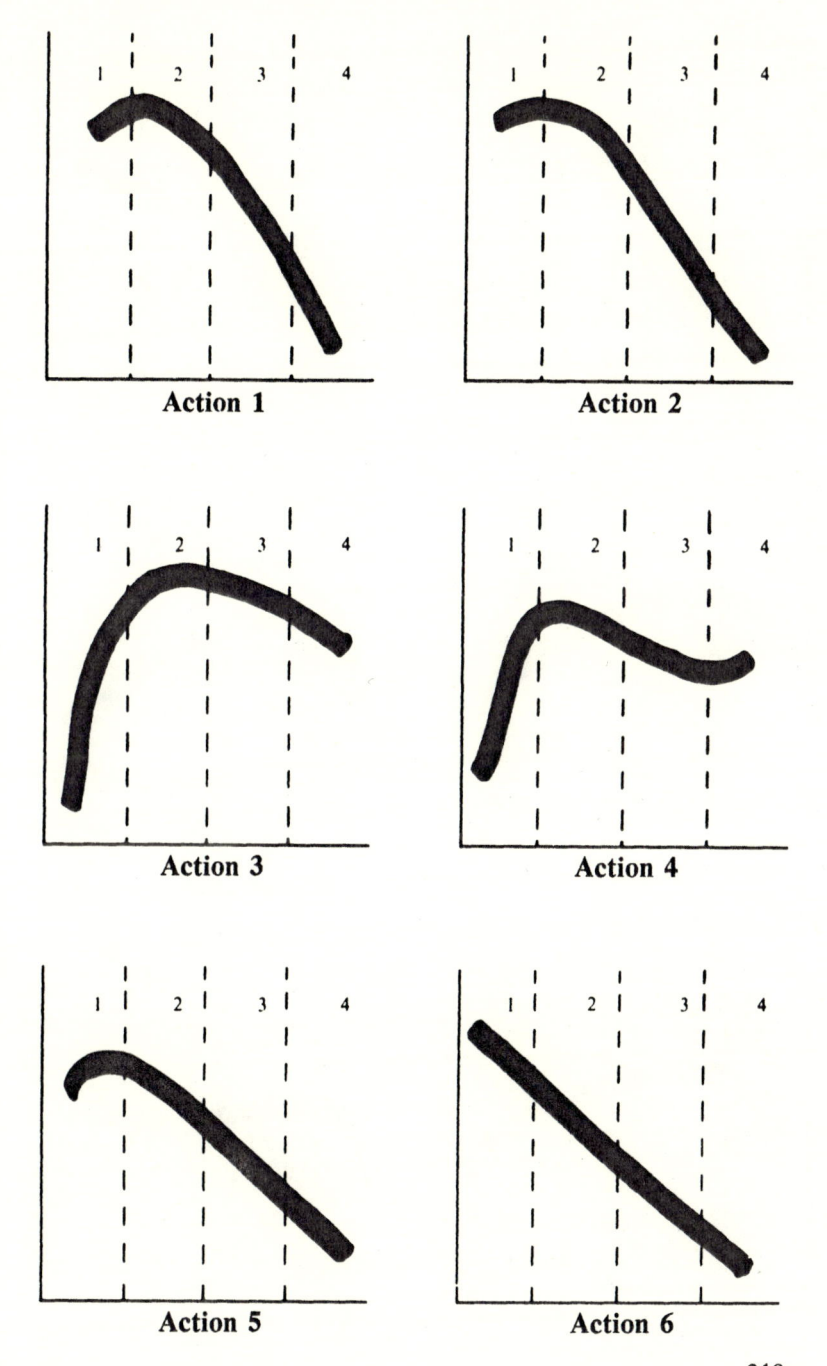

**Action 2**

**Action 3**

**Action 4**

**Action 5**

**Action 6**

Action 7

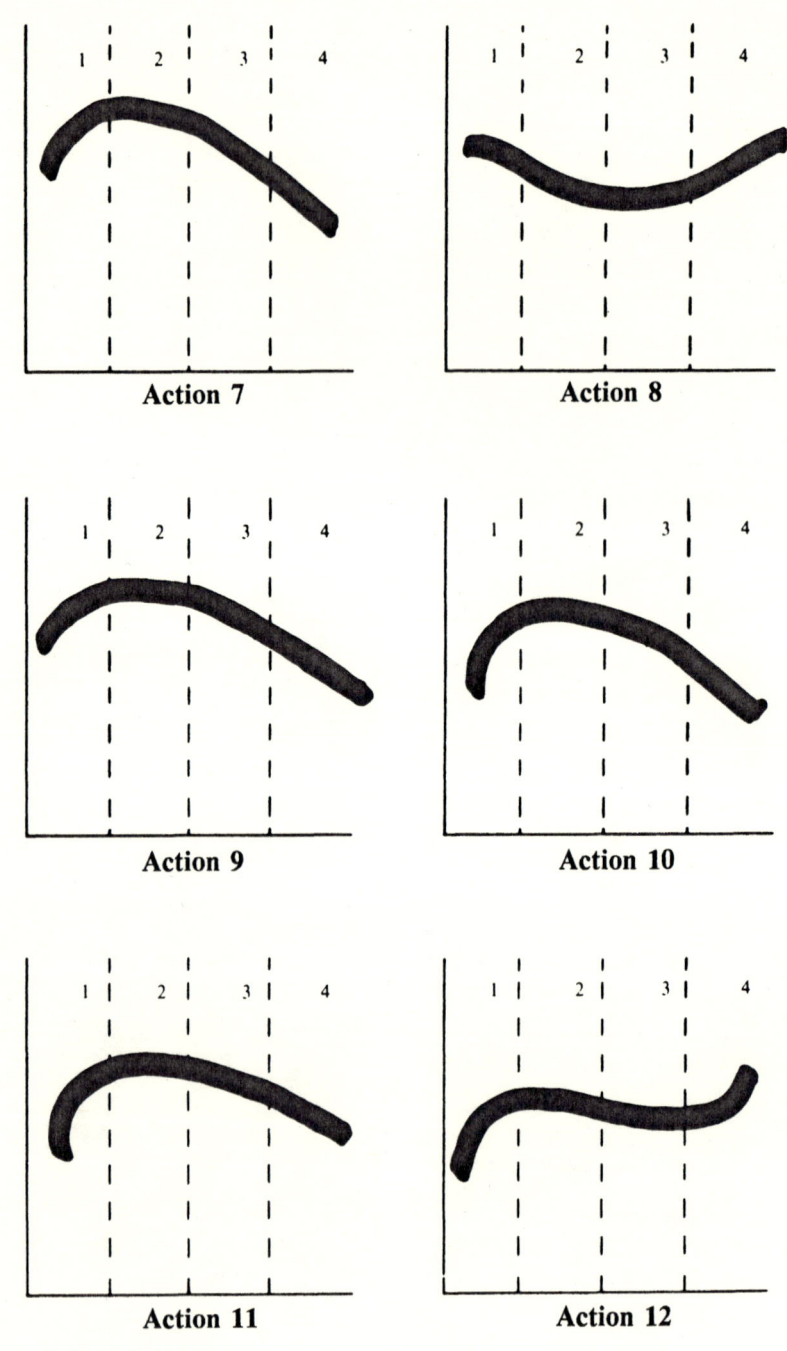

Action 8

Action 9

Action 10

Action 11

Action 12

220

**Action 13**

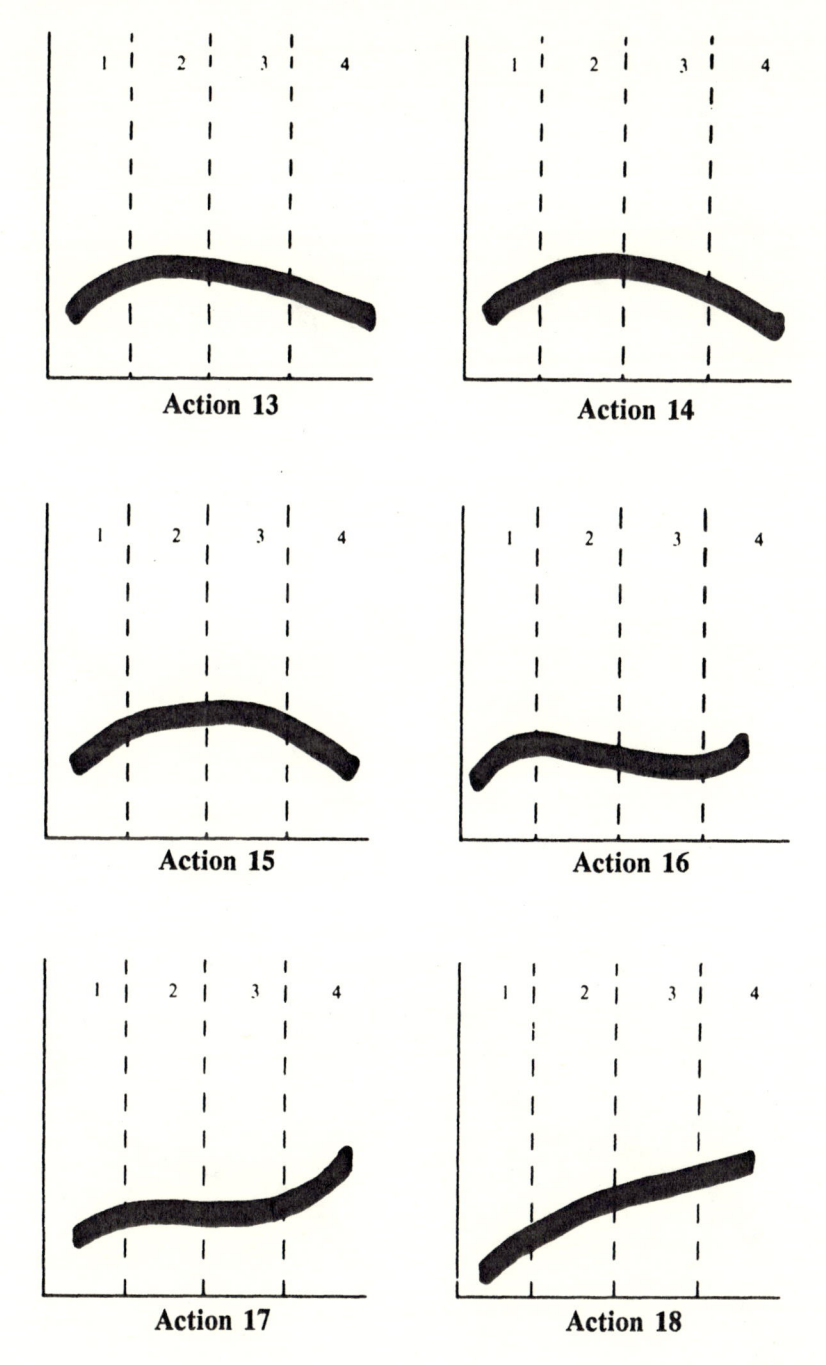

**Action 14**

**Action 15**

**Action 16**

**Action 17**

**Action 18**

Action 19

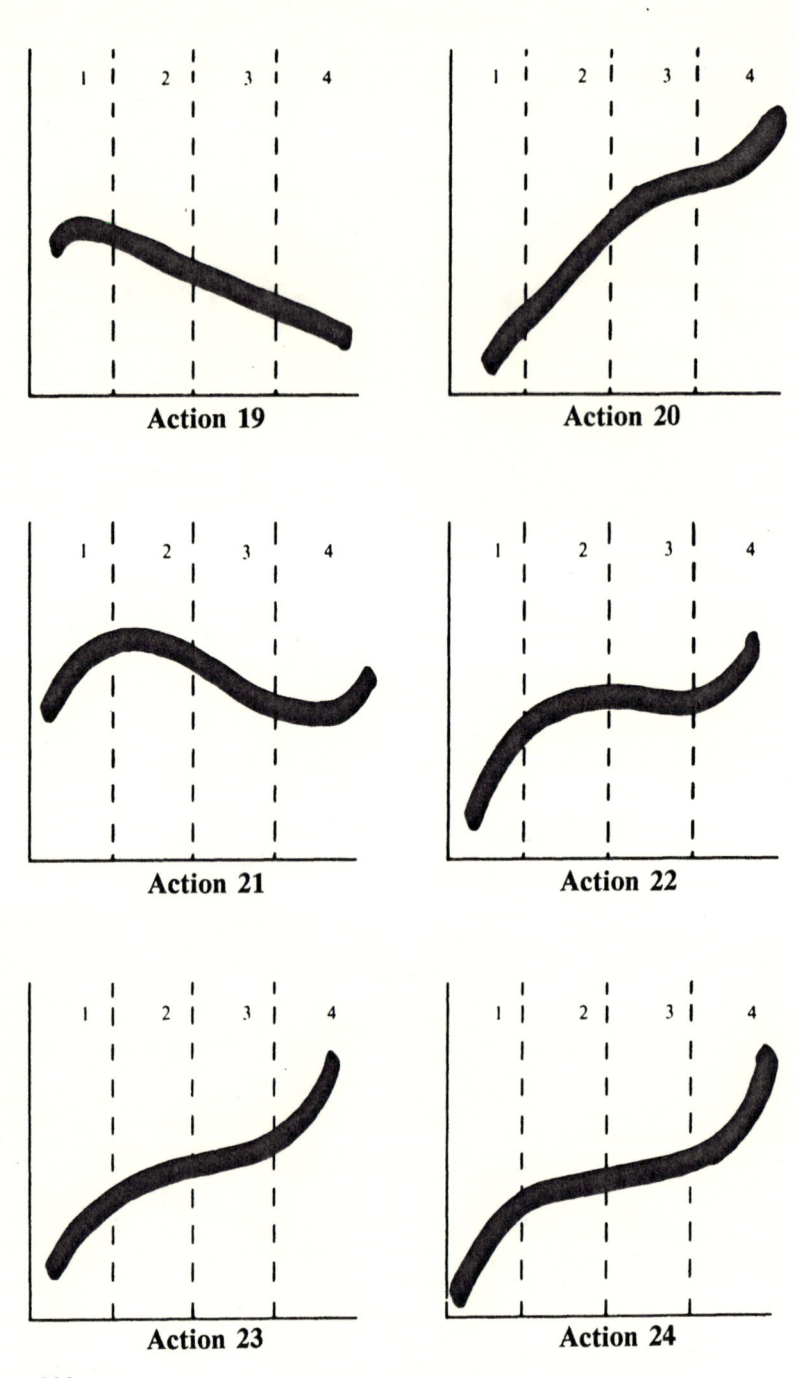

Action 20

Action 21

Action 22

Action 23

Action 24

**Action 25**

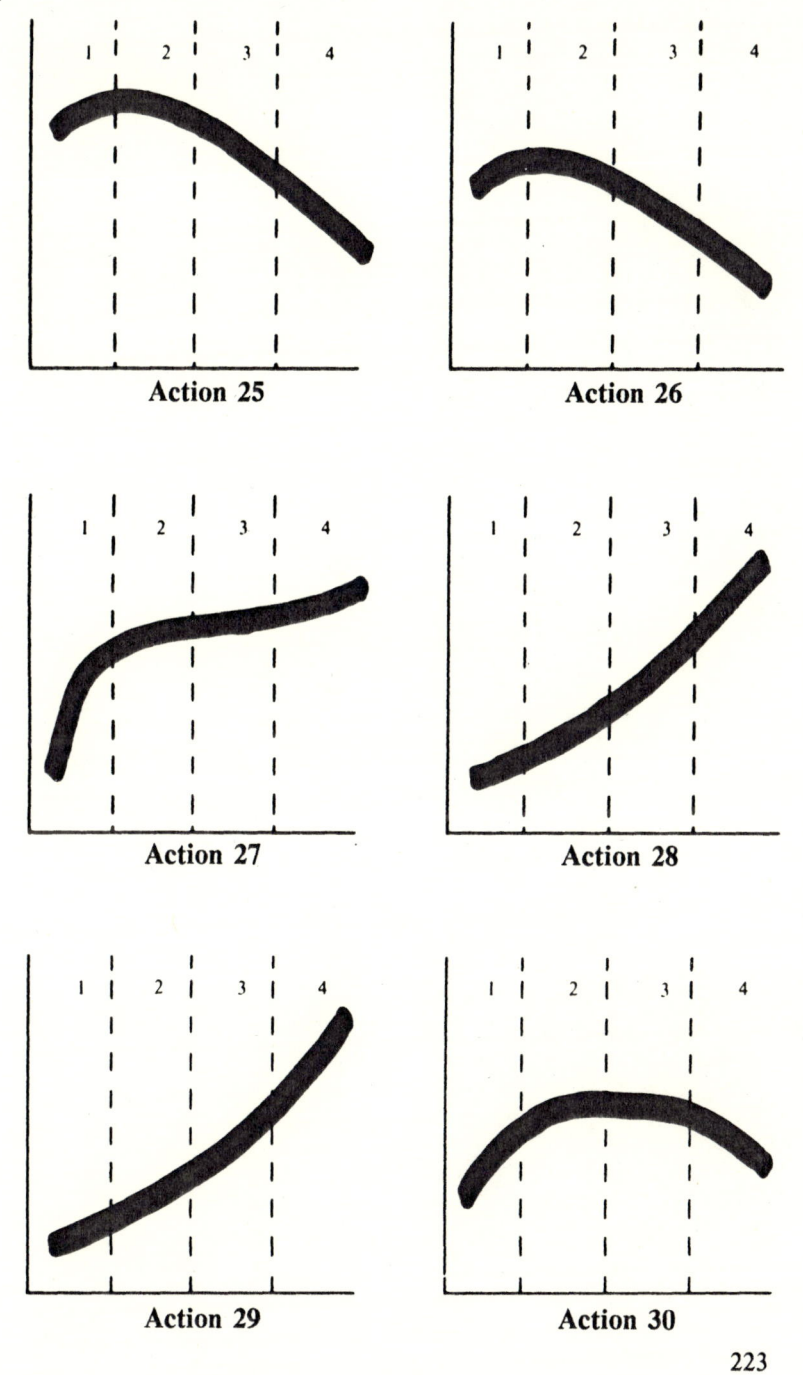

**Action 26**

**Action 27**

**Action 28**

**Action 29**

**Action 30**

**Action 31**

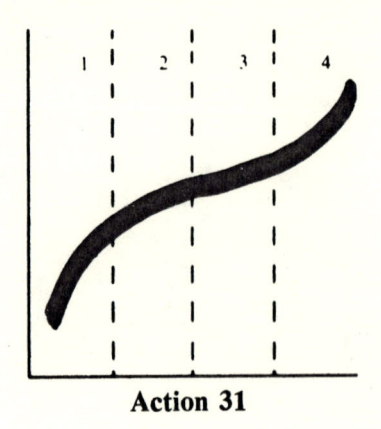

# INDEX

NOTE: The specific symptoms, tools, and remedial actions discussed in this book are identified by number on pages 205–212.

Assembly operations:
  in basic business, 179
  in marginal business, 181
Assignment of discrete tasks, 126–127

Capacity, reduction of, 177–180
Capacity utilization improvement, 180–185
Cash payment for marginal business ("cash on the barrelhead"), 183
Cash flow forecasts, 42–44
  excessive precision of, 43–44
Communication, importance of:
  with market segments, 131–132
  with operating organization, 130–131
Components versus finished goods, 181–182
Cost reduction: *see* Reduction of costs
Costs, nature of, 123–124

Decision criteria for turnaround action, 123–127
Direct sale of components, 182
Dynamic margin, 99–101

Engineering content simplification, 181
Engineering expense, 58–67
Expense reduction: *see* Reduction of expenses
Expenses, nature of, 125–126

225

Fabrication operations, 179
Flexible delivery of parts, 184
Focusing on operations, 185
Four stages in turnaround situations:
   Stage 1 (cash crunch), 20
   Stage 2 (cash shortfall), 20
   Stage 3 (quantity of profit), 21
   Stage 4 (quality of profit), 21

Inflow-outflow questions, 40

Logical inference, 4–5

Management, direction of, 128
"Management by thrashabout," 29
Marginal business, 180–185
Market segment or distribution channel, 97
Motivation and monitoring of operating organization, 192–197

OEM (original equipment manufacturing) sales, 182

Packing, in plain brown wrapper, 184
Pareto's law, 43, 70
Percent of sales ratios, 101–119
Plant capacity, definition, 117
Precision of fabrication in marginal business, 183–184
Pricing strategies, 169–171
Product pruning, 162–163

Profit improvement, definition, 125
Profitability improvement, definition, 125

Raw material inventory for marginal business, 183
Reasoning skills, 5–6
Reduction of costs, 124, 173–185
Reduction of expenses:
   people-related, 145–155
   plant-related, 158–161
   product-related, 155–158

Sales improvement as short-term strategy, 167–172
Segregation accounting, 183
Symptom identification and measurement, principles of, 40

"Three perpetual problems" (as seen by market), 132
Three P's of cash/profit flow, 13–19
   people, 14–15
   plant, 17–19
   product, 15–17

Turnaround cycle, length of, 182–183
Turnaround plan, 189–191

Unit burden expense, 52–58
Unitization of measurements, 40
Unprofitable business, 161–167

Work-load criteria, 153

Printed in the United States
1356400001B/296